ΣΟΦΟΚΛΕΟΥΣ SOPHOCLES'
Φιλοκτήτης *Philoctetes*

A Dual Language Edition

Greek Text Edited by
Francis Storr

English Translation and Notes by
Ian Johnston

Edited by
Evan Hayes and Stephen Nimis

FAENUM PUBLISHING
OXFORD, OHIO

Sophocles Philoctetes: *A Dual Language Edition*
First Edition

© 2017 by Faenum Publishing

ISBN-10: 1940997941
ISBN-13: 9781940997940

Published by Faenum Publishing, Ltd.
Cover Design: Evan Hayes

for Geoffrey (1974-1997)

οἴη περ φύλλων γενεὴ τοίη δὲ καὶ ἀνδρῶν.
φύλλα τὰ μέν τ᾽ ἄνεμος χαμάδις χέει, ἄλλα δέ θ᾽ ὕλη
τηλεθόωσα φύει, ἔαρος δ᾽ ἐπιγίγνεται ὥρη:
ὡς ἀνδρῶν γενεὴ ἣ μὲν φύει ἣ δ᾽ ἀπολήγει.

Generations of men are like the leaves.
In winter, winds blow them down to earth,
but then, when spring season comes again,
the budding wood grows more. And so with men:
one generation grows, another dies away.   (*Iliad* 6)

TABLE OF CONTENTS

EDITORS' NOTE

This volume presents the Ancient Greek text of Sophocles' *Philoctetes* with a facing English translation. The Greek text is that of Francis Storr, which is in the public domain and available as a pdf. This text has also been digitized by the Perseus Project (perseus.tufts.edu). The English translation and accompanying notes are those of Ian Johnston of Vancouver Island University, Nanaimo, BC. This translation is available freely online (records.viu.ca/~johnstoi/). We have reset both texts, making a number of very minor corrections and modifications, and placed them on opposing pages. This facing-page format will be useful to those wishing to read the English translation while looking at version of the Greek original, or vice versa.

Occasionally readings from other editions of or commentaries on Sophocles' Greek text are used, accounting for some minor departures from Storr. Even so, some small discrepancies exist between the Greek text and the English translation.

MYTHOLOGICAL BACKGROUND

Philoctetes was one of the warrior leaders who set off with Agamemnon and Menelaus to attack Troy. On the way he was bitten by a snake, and the wound refused to heal. His cries of pain and the stench of his wound so upset the Greeks that the leaders decided to abandon him on the deserted island of Lemnos, where he remained all by himself. The action of the play takes place ten years after this event.

ΦΙΛΟΚΤΗΤΗΣ

PHILOCTETES

ΤΑ ΤΟΥ ΔΡΑΜΑΤΟΣ ΠΡΟΣΩΠΑ

ΟΔΥΣΣΕΥΣ

ΝΕΟΠΤΟΛΕΜΟΣ

ΦΙΛΟΚΤΗΤΗΣ

ΣΚΟΠΟΣ

ΧΟΡΟΣ

ΕΜΠΟΡΟΣ

ΗΡΑΚΛΗΣ

DRAMATIS PERSONAE

ODYSSEUS: king of Ithaca, a leading warrior of the Greek army at Troy.

NEOPTOLEMUS: young son of the great Greek hero Achilles.

PHILOCTETES: Greek warrior abandon on Lemnos.

SAILOR: attendant on Neoptolemus.

CHORUS: sailors from Neoptolemus' ship.[1]

MERCHANT TRADER: a sailor spy, posing as a Merchant.

HERCULES: mortal son of Zeus, later made a god.

Φιλοκτήτης

ΟΔΥΣΣΕΥΣ

ἀκτὴ μὲν ἥδε τῆς περιρρύτου χθονὸς
Λήμνου, βροτοῖς ἄστιπτος οὐδ' οἰκουμένη,
ἔνθ', ὦ κρατίστου πατρὸς Ἑλλήνων τραφεὶς
Ἀχιλλέως παῖ Νεοπτόλεμε, τὸν Μηλιᾶ
Ποίαντος υἱὸν ἐξέθηκ' ἐγώ ποτε,   5
ταχθεὶς τόδ' ἔρδειν τῶν ἀνασσόντων ὕπο,
νόσῳ καταστάζοντα διαβόρῳ πόδα·
ὅτ' οὔτε λοιβῆς ἡμὶν οὔτε θυμάτων
παρῆν ἑκήλοις προσθιγεῖν, ἀλλ' ἀγρίαις
κατεῖχ' ἀεὶ πᾶν στρατόπεδον δυσφημίαις,   10
βοῶν, στενάζων. ἀλλὰ ταῦτα μὲν τί δεῖ
λέγειν; ἀκμὴ γὰρ οὐ μακρῶν ἡμῖν λόγων,
μὴ καὶ μάθῃ μ' ἥκοντα κἀκχέω τὸ πᾶν
σόφισμα, τῷ νιν αὐτίχ' αἱρήσειν δοκῶ.
ἀλλ' ἔργον ἤδη σὸν τὰ λοίφ' ὑπηρετεῖν   15
σκοπεῖν θ' ὅπου 'στ' ἐνταῦθα δίστομος πέτρα
τοιάδ', ἵν' ἐν ψύχει μὲν ἡλίου διπλῆ
πάρεστιν ἐνθάκησις, ἐν θέρει δ' ὕπνον
δι' ἀμφιτρῆτος αὐλίου πέμπει πνοή·
βαιὸν δ' ἔνερθεν ἐξ ἀριστερᾶς τάχ' ἂν   20
ἴδοις ποτὸν κρηναῖον, εἴπερ ἐστὶ σῶν.
ἅ μοι προσελθὼν σῖγα σήμαιν' εἴτ' ἐκεῖ
χῶρον τὸν αὐτὸν τόνδ' ἔτ' εἴτ' ἄλλῃ κυρεῖ,
ὡς τἀπίλοιπα τῶν λόγων σὺ μὲν κλύῃς,
ἐγὼ δὲ φράζω, κοινὰ δ' ἐξ ἀμφοῖν ἴῃ.   25

Philoctetes

[Scene: on the deserted island of Lemnos, just outside Philoctetes' cave. The opening to the cave is on stage, above the level of the orchestra. Enter into the orchestra ODYSSEUS and NEOPTOLEMUS with a SAILOR attending on Neoptolemus]

ODYSSEUS

    So here we are on the shores of Lemnos,
    a lonely place—well off the beaten track,
    surrounded by the sea. No one lives here.
    This was this place, Neoptolemus,
    son of Achilles, bravest and best
    of all the Greeks, where, many years ago,
    I left Philoctetes, son of Poeas,
    a man from Malis. I abandoned him,
    acting on orders from our two commanders.[2]
    His foot was dripping with infectious sores,
    painful ulcers. He kept screaming all the time.
    His strange, wild howling rang throughout the camp.   [10]
    He cried so much we could not pray in peace
    or make libations and burnt sacrifice.
    But what's the point in talking of that now?
    This is no time to tell long stories,
    for if he learns I'm here, then my whole scheme,
    the one I think will catch him quickly, fails.
    Look, your job is to carry out the tasks
    we still have left to do—to find a rock
    somewhere round here which has two openings,
    so shaped that when it's cool there are two seats
    facing the sun, and when it's hot, the breeze
    wafts sleep in through the chamber tunnel.
    To the left below it you might glimpse   [20]
    a water spring, if it's still functioning.
    Climb up the rock. Keep quiet. Then signal me,
    if you see those features there or somewhere else.
    After that I'll tell you my entire plan.
    Then both of us will carry out my scheme.

Sophocles

ΝΕΟΠΤΟΛΕΜΟΣ
ἄναξ Ὀδυσσεῦ, τοὔργον οὐ μακρὰν λέγεις·
δοκῶ γὰρ οἷον εἶπας ἄντρον εἰσορᾶν.

ΟΔΥΣΣΕΥΣ
ἄνωθεν ἢ κάτωθεν; οὐ γὰρ ἐννοῶ.

ΝΕΟΠΤΟΛΕΜΟΣ
τόδ᾽ ἐξύπερθε· καὶ στίβου γ᾽ οὐδεὶς κτύπος.

ΟΔΥΣΣΕΥΣ
ὅρα καθ᾽ ὕπνον μὴ καταυλισθεὶς κυρεῖ.　　　　30

ΝΕΟΠΤΟΛΕΜΟΣ
ὁρῶ κενὴν οἴκησιν ἀνθρώπων δίχα.

ΟΔΥΣΣΕΥΣ
οὐδ᾽ ἔνδον οἰκοποιός ἐστί τις τροφή;

ΝΕΟΠΤΟΛΕΜΟΣ
στιπτή γε φυλλὰς ὡς ἐναυλίζοντί τῳ.

ΟΔΥΣΣΕΥΣ
τὰ δ᾽ ἄλλ᾽ ἔρημα, κοὐδέν ἐσθ᾽ ὑπόστεγον;

ΝΕΟΠΤΟΛΕΜΟΣ
αὐτόξυλόν γ᾽ ἔκπωμα, φλαυρουργοῦ τινος　　　　35
τεχνήματ᾽ ἀνδρός, καὶ πυρεῖ᾽ ὁμοῦ τάδε.

ΟΔΥΣΣΕΥΣ
κείνου τὸ θησαύρισμα σημαίνεις τόδε.

ΝΕΟΠΤΟΛΕΜΟΣ
ἰοὺ ἰού· καὶ ταῦτά γ᾽ ἄλλα θάλπεται
ῥάκη, βαρείας του νοσηλείας πλέα.

6

[NEOPTOLEMUS sets out searching, moving up towards the opening of the cave]

NEOPTOLEMUS
    Lord Odysseus, that task you mentioned—
    I think we're close. I see a cave up here
    quite like the one you mentioned.

ODYSSEUS
                              Above you?
    Or below? I don't see it.

NEOPTOLEMUS *[approaching the mouth of the cave]*
                                    It's up here.
    High up. I can't hear a sound—no footsteps.

ODYSSEUS
    Watch out. He may be there, in bed asleep.   [30]

NEOPTOLEMUS *[peering into the cave]*
    The place is empty. I don't see anyone.

ODYSSEUS
    Anything in there which might indicate
    some human lives inside?

NEOPTOLEMUS
                                    Yes, there is—
    a bed of leaves pressed down. Someone lives here.

ODYSSEUS
    Is it empty otherwise? Nothing else
    hidden in the cave?

NEOPTOLEMUS
                        There's a wooden cup,
    crudely made, some wretched craftsman's work—
    and kindling, too, set to light a fire.

ODYSSEUS
    What you describe must be the things he owns.

NEOPTOLEMUS
    Look here, there's something else. Rags left to dry—

[NEOPTOLEMUS inspects the rags]

    Agh, they're full of pus! The stench!

Sophocles

ΟΔΥΣΣΕΥΣ

  ἀνὴρ κατοικεῖ τούσδε τοὺς τόπους σαφῶς,   40
  κἄστ' οὐχ ἑκάς που· πῶς γὰρ ἂν νοσῶν ἀνὴρ
  κῶλον παλαιᾷ κηρὶ προσβαίη μακράν;
  ἀλλ' ἢ 'πὶ φορβῆς νόστον ἐξελήλυθεν
  ἢ φύλλον εἴ τι νώδυνον κάτοιδέ που.
  τὸν οὖν παρόντα πέμψον εἰς κατασκοπήν,   45
  μὴ καὶ λάθῃ με προσπεσών· ὡς μᾶλλον ἂν
  ἕλοιτό μ' ἢ τοὺς πάντας Ἀργείους λαβεῖν.

ΝΕΟΠΤΟΛΕΜΟΣ

  ἀλλ' ἔρχεταί τε καὶ φυλάξεται στίβος.
  σὺ δ', εἴ τι χρῄζεις, φράζε δευτέρῳ λόγῳ.

ΟΔΥΣΣΕΥΣ

  Ἀχιλλέως παῖ, δεῖ σ' ἐφ' οἷς ἐλήλυθας   50
  γενναῖον εἶναι, μὴ μόνον τῷ σώματι,
  ἀλλ' ἤν τι καινὸν ὧν πρὶν οὐκ ἀκήκοας
  κλύῃς, ὑπουργεῖν, ὡς ὑπηρέτης πάρει.

ΝΕΟΠΤΟΛΕΜΟΣ

  τί δῆτ' ἄνωγας;

ΟΔΥΣΣΕΥΣ

          τὴν Φιλοκτήτου σε δεῖ
  ψυχὴν ὅπως δόλοισιν ἐκκλέψεις λέγων.   55
  ὅταν σ' ἐρωτᾷ τίς τε καὶ πόθεν πάρει,
  λέγειν, Ἀχιλλέως παῖς· τόδ' οὐχὶ κλεπτέον·
  πλεῖς δ' ὡς πρὸς οἶκον, ἐκλιπὼν τὸ ναυτικὸν
  στράτευμ' Ἀχαιῶν, ἔχθος ἐχθήρας μέγα,
  οἵ σ' ἐν λιταῖς στείλαντες ἐξ οἴκων μολεῖν,   60
  μόνην ἔχοντες τήνδ' ἅλωσιν Ἰλίου,
  οὐκ ἠξίωσαν τῶν Ἀχιλλείων ὅπλων
  ἐλθόντι δοῦναι κυρίως αἰτουμένῳ,
  ἀλλ' αὔτ' Ὀδυσσεῖ παρέδοσαν· λέγων ὅσ' ἂν
  θέλῃς καθ' ἡμῶν ἔσχατ' ἐσχάτων κακά.   65

ODYSSEUS
                                        This is the spot.
Obviously our man lives here and is nearby.   [40]
His foot is crippled with that old disease.
He can't go far. He's gone to find some food
or a remedial herb he's seen somewhere.
Send that man of yours to be our lookout,
in case he stumbles on us unawares.
He'd rather catch me than any other Greek.

*[NEOPTOLEMUS comes back down and whispers to his ATTENDANT,
who then leaves]*

NEOPTOLEMUS
He's on his way. He'll be our sentry on the path.
If there's something else you need, just say so.

ODYSSEUS
Son of Achilles, to fulfill your mission,   [50]
you must be loyal to your ancestry.
That's more than something merely physical.
If you hear a plan you've not heard before
and it sounds strange, you must obey it—
you're with me here as my subordinate.

NEOPTOLEMUS
What are your orders?

ODYSSEUS
                            With Philoctetes—
when you speak to him, tell him a story.
You have to trick him, lead his mind astray.
When he asks who you are and where you're from,
say you're Achilles' son—no deception there.
But tell him you intend to sail for home.
You've left the Achaeans' naval forces
because you truly hate them. And here's why—
in their prayers they summoned you from home   [60]
to Troy, since you're the only hope they've got
to take the city. But then they judged you
not good enough to have Achilles' arms,
although you came to claim them as your right.
Instead they gave them to Odysseus.
Say what you like of me—pile up the insults,

τούτῳ γὰρ οὐδέν μ' ἀλγυνεῖς· εἰ δ' ἐργάσει
μὴ ταῦτα, λύπην πᾶσιν Ἀργείοις βαλεῖς.
εἰ γὰρ τὰ τοῦδε τόξα μὴ ληφθήσεται,
οὐκ ἔστι πέρσαι σοι τὸ Δαρδάνου πέδον.
ὡς δ' ἔστ' ἐμοὶ μὲν οὐχί, σοὶ δ' ὁμιλία   70
πρὸς τόνδε πιστὴ καὶ βέβαιος, ἔκμαθε.
σὺ μὲν πέπλευκας οὔτ' ἔνορκος οὐδενὶ
οὔτ' ἐξ ἀνάγκης οὔτε τοῦ πρώτου στόλου·
ἐμοὶ δὲ τούτων οὐδέν ἐστ' ἀρνήσιμον.
ὥστ' εἴ με τόξων ἐγκρατὴς αἰσθήσεται,   75
ὄλωλα καὶ σὲ προσδιαφθερῶ ξυνών.
ἀλλ' αὐτὸ τοῦτο δεῖ σοφισθῆναι, κλοπεὺς
ὅπως γενήσει τῶν ἀνικήτων ὅπλων.
ἔξοιδα, παῖ, φύσει σε μὴ πεφυκότα
τοιαῦτα φωνεῖν μηδὲ τεχνᾶσθαι κακά·   80
ἀλλ' ἡδὺ γάρ τι κτῆμα τῆς νίκης λαβεῖν,
τόλμα· δίκαιοι δ' αὖθις ἐκφανούμεθα.
νῦν δ' εἰς ἀναιδὲς ἡμέρας μέρος βραχὺ
δός μοι σεαυτόν, κᾆτα τὸν λοιπὸν χρόνον
κέκλησο πάντων εὐσεβέστατος βροτῶν.   85

ΝΕΟΠΤΟΛΕΜΟΣ

ἐγὼ μὲν οὓς ἂν τῶν λόγων ἀλγῶ κλύων,
Λαερτίου παῖ, τούσδε καὶ πράσσειν στυγῶ·
ἔφυν γὰρ οὐδὲν ἐκ τέχνης πράσσειν κακῆς,
οὔτ' αὐτὸς οὔθ', ὥς φασιν, οὑκφύσας ἐμέ.
ἀλλ' εἴμ' ἕτοιμος πρὸς βίαν τὸν ἄνδρ' ἄγειν   90
καὶ μὴ δόλοισιν· οὐ γὰρ ἐξ ἑνὸς ποδὸς
ἡμᾶς τοσούσδε πρὸς βίαν χειρώσεται.
πεμφθείς γε μέντοι σοὶ ξυνεργάτης ὀκνῶ
προδότης καλεῖσθαι· βούλομαι δ', ἄναξ, καλῶς
δρῶν ἐξαμαρτεῖν μᾶλλον ἢ νικᾶν κακῶς.   95

the worst there are. That won't injure me.
But if you don't go through with what I say,
you'll hurt the Argives, every one of them.
If we don't get our hands on that man's bow,
you'll never capture Troy successfully,
never destroy the realm of Dardanus.[3]
Let me tell you why you can talk to him   [70]
and safely win his trust, while I cannot.
You've joined the Trojan expedition freely—
you'd made no oath to anyone. In fact,
you weren't a member of that first contingent.[4]
But I was, and I can't deny the fact.
If he sees me while he still has his bow,
I'm lost, and you, as my companion,
will share my fate. That's why we need to plan—
we need some scheme so you can find a way
to steal his bow, which is invincible.
My boy, I know your nature is not fit
to make up lies or speak deceitful things.   [80]
But winning victory's prize is sweet indeed,
so force yourself to do it. After this,
the justice of our actions will be clear.
So now, for one short day, follow my lead
without a sense of shame. In time to come
they will call you the finest man there is.

NEOPTOLEMUS

Son of Laertes, I hate to carry out
an order which it hurts to listen to.
It's not my nature to do anything
based on deceit. My father, so they say,
was just the same. But I am prepared   [90]
to take the man by force, no trickery.
He's just one man on foot. He'll never win
against so many of us in a fight.
Since I was ordered here to work with you,
I am not eager to be called disloyal.
Still, my lord, I would much prefer to fail
in something honorable, than to win out
with treachery.

Sophocles

ΟΔΥΣΣΕΥΣ

ἐσθλοῦ πατρὸς παῖ, καὐτὸς ὢν νέος ποτὲ
γλῶσσαν μὲν ἀργόν, χεῖρα δ᾽ εἶχον ἐργάτιν·
νῦν δ᾽ εἰς ἔλεγχον ἐξιὼν ὁρῶ βροτοῖς
τὴν γλῶσσαν, οὐχὶ τἄργα, πάνθ᾽ ἡγουμένην.

ΝΕΟΠΤΟΛΕΜΟΣ

τί μ᾽ οὖν ἄνωγας ἄλλο πλὴν ψευδῆ λέγειν;   100

ΟΔΥΣΣΕΥΣ

λέγω σ᾽ ἐγὼ δόλῳ Φιλοκτήτην λαβεῖν.

ΝΕΟΠΤΟΛΕΜΟΣ

τί δ᾽ ἐν δόλῳ δεῖ μᾶλλον ἢ πείσαντ᾽ ἄγειν;

ΟΔΥΣΣΕΥΣ

οὐ μὴ πίθηται· πρὸς βίαν δ᾽ οὐκ ἂν λάβοις.

ΝΕΟΠΤΟΛΕΜΟΣ

οὕτως ἔχει τι δεινὸν ἰσχύος θράσος;

ΟΔΥΣΣΕΥΣ

ἰοὺς γ᾽ ἀφύκτους καὶ προπέμποντας φόνον.   105

ΝΕΟΠΤΟΛΕΜΟΣ

οὐκ ἆρ᾽ ἐκείνῳ γ᾽ οὐδὲ προσμῖξαι θρασύ;

ΟΔΥΣΣΕΥΣ

οὔ, μὴ δόλῳ λαβόντα γ᾽, ὡς ἐγὼ λέγω.

ΝΕΟΠΤΟΛΕΜΟΣ

οὐκ αἰσχρὸν ἡγεῖ δῆτα τὸ ψευδῆ λέγειν;

ΟΔΥΣΣΕΥΣ

οὔκ, εἰ τὸ σωθῆναί γε τὸ ψεῦδος φέρει.

ΝΕΟΠΤΟΛΕΜΟΣ

πῶς οὖν βλέπων τις ταῦτα τολμήσει λακεῖν;   110

12

ODYSSEUS
You noble father's son,
when I was young, I had a quiet tongue, as well.
I let my active hands speak up for me.
But now I've gone out into adult life
and faced its trials, I see with mortal men
the tongue, not action, rules in everything.

NEOPTOLEMUS
What are your orders, then, apart from lying?   [100]

ODYSSEUS
I'm ordering you to use deceitful means
to seize Philoctetes.

NEOPTOLEMUS
But why deceit?
Why not persuade him?

ODYSSEUS
The man won't listen.
And he's not someone you can take by force.

NEOPTOLEMUS
Is he that confident, that powerful?

ODYSSEUS
Indeed, he is. His arrows never miss.
Every shot brings death.

NEOPTOLEMUS
I have no chance at all
if I move out to challenge him?

ODYSSEUS
None whatsoever, unless, as I've said,
you use some trick to grab him.

NEOPTOLEMUS
So you don't think
there's any shame in saying something false?

ODYSSEUS
No, I don't—not if the lies will save us.

NEOPTOLEMUS
But how can anyone control his face   [110]
when he dares speak such lies?

Sophocles

ΟΔΥΣΣΕΥΣ
ὅταν τι δρᾷς εἰς κέρδος, οὐκ ὀκνεῖν πρέπει.

ΝΕΟΠΤΟΛΕΜΟΣ
κέρδος δ᾽ ἐμοὶ τί τοῦτον ἐς Τροίαν μολεῖν;

ΟΔΥΣΣΕΥΣ
αἱρεῖ τὰ τόξα ταῦτα τὴν Τροίαν μόνα.

ΝΕΟΠΤΟΛΕΜΟΣ
οὐκ ἆρ᾽ ὁ πέρσων, ὡς ἐφάσκετ᾽, εἴμ᾽ ἐγώ;

ΟΔΥΣΣΕΥΣ
οὔτ᾽ ἂν σὺ κείνων χωρὶς οὔτ᾽ ἐκεῖνα σοῦ.   115

ΝΕΟΠΤΟΛΕΜΟΣ
θηρατέ᾽ οὖν γίγνοιτ᾽ ἄν, εἴπερ ὧδ᾽ ἔχει.

ΟΔΥΣΣΕΥΣ
ὡς τοῦτό γ᾽ ἔρξας δύο φέρει δωρήματα.

ΝΕΟΠΤΟΛΕΜΟΣ
ποίω; μαθὼν γὰρ οὐκ ἂν ἀρνοίμην τὸ δρᾶν.

ΟΔΥΣΣΕΥΣ
σοφός τ᾽ ἂν αὑτὸς κἀγαθὸς κεκλῇ᾽ ἅμα.

ΝΕΟΠΤΟΛΕΜΟΣ
ἴτω· ποήσω, πᾶσαν αἰσχύνην ἀφείς.   120

ΟΔΥΣΣΕΥΣ
ἦ μνημονεύεις οὖν ἅ σοι παρήνεσα;

ΝΕΟΠΤΟΛΕΜΟΣ
σάφ᾽ ἴσθ᾽, ἐπείπερ εἰσάπαξ συνῄνεσα.

ΟΔΥΣΣΕΥΣ
σὺ μὲν μένων νυν κεῖνον ἐνθάδ᾽ ἐκδέχου,
ἐγὼ δ᾽ ἄπειμι, μὴ κατοπτευθῶ παρών,

14

ODYSSEUS
                         When what you do
  brings benefits, you should not hesitate.

NEOPTOLEMUS
  If that man comes to Troy, how do I benefit?

ODYSSEUS
  The only way the city can be captured
  is with his bow and arrows.

NEOPTOLEMUS
                         So I am not the one
  who'll take that city, as you told me?

ODYSSEUS
  Yes, but you need them, and they need you.⁵

NEOPTOLEMUS
  If that's true, we must track them down, it seems.

ODYSSEUS
  By doing this work, you'll garner two rewards.

NEOPTOLEMUS
  How? If I knew that, I'd not refuse it.

ODYSSEUS
  In this one act, you'll get yourself a name
  for shrewdness and nobility.

NEOPTOLEMUS
                         All right,   [120]
  I'll do it. I'll set all shame aside.

ODYSSEUS
  That story I sketched out for you just now—
  do you recall it?

NEOPTOLEMUS
                         You can be sure of that,
  since I've at last agreed to do it.

ODYSSEUS
  All right. Now, you stay here and wait for him.
  I'll move off, so I'm not seen around you.

Sophocles

καὶ τὸν σκοπὸν πρὸς ναῦν ἀποστελῶ πάλιν.   125
καὶ δεῦρ', ἐάν μοι τοῦ χρόνου δοκῆτέ τι
κατασχολάζειν, αὖθις ἐκπέμψω πάλιν
τοῦτον τὸν αὐτὸν ἄνδρα, ναυκλήρου τρόποις
μορφὴν δολώσας, ὡς ἂν ἀγνοίᾳ προσῇ·
οὗ δῆτα, τέκνον, ποικίλως αὐδωμένου   130
δέχου τὰ συμφέροντα τῶν ἀεὶ λόγων.
ἐγὼ δὲ πρὸς ναῦν εἶμι, σοὶ παρεὶς τάδε·
Ἑρμῆς δ' ὁ πέμπων δόλιος ἡγήσαιτο νῷν
Νίκη τ' Ἀθάνα Πολιάς, ἣ σῴζει μ' ἀεί.

ΧΟΡΟΣ

τί χρὴ τί χρή με, δέσποτ', ἐν ξένᾳ ξένον   135
στέγειν ἢ τί λέγειν πρὸς ἄνδρ' ὑπόπταν;
φράζε μοι. τέχνα γὰρ
τέχνας ἑτέρας προύχει
καὶ γνώμα παρ' ὅτῳ τὸ θεῖον
Διὸς σκῆπτρον ἀνάσσεται.   140
σὲ δ', ὦ τέκνον, τόδ' ἐλήλυθεν
πᾶν κράτος ὠγύγιον· τό μοι ἔννεπε
τί σοι χρεὼν ὑπουργεῖν.

ΝΕΟΠΤΟΛΕΜΟΣ

νῦν μέν, ἴσως γὰρ τόπον ἐσχατιαῖς
προσιδεῖν ἐθέλεις ὅντινα κεῖται,   145
δέρκου θαρσῶν· ὁπόταν δὲ μόλῃ
δεινὸς ὁδίτης, τῶνδ' οὐκ μελάθρων
πρὸς ἐμὴν αἰεὶ χεῖρα προχωρῶν
πειρῶ τὸ παρὸν θεραπεύειν.

ΧΟΡΟΣ

μέλον πάλαι μέλημά μοι λέγεις, ἄναξ,   150
φρουρεῖν ὄμμ' ἐπὶ σῷ μάλιστα καιρῷ·

16

And I'll return our lookout to his ship.
Now, if I think you're taking too much time,
I'll send that same sailor here again,
but I'll disguise his actions and his clothes,
to make him captain of some merchant ship,
beyond all recognition. Then, my boy,   [130]
when he tells you some fancy tale, you listen,
taking from it anything that helps you.
Now I'm going to my ship. It's up to you.
May Hermes, who guides men through deceptions,
lead us through this, and with Athena, too,
goddess of victory, our city's patron,
and the one who always rescues me.

[Exit ODYSSEUS. Enter the CHORUS, members of Neoptolemus' crew]

CHORUS
My lord, tell me what I must conceal
and what to say to this Philoctetes.
He's bound to be full of suspicion.
For I'm a stranger in a foreign place.
The art and judgment of the man
who rules with Zeus' godlike sceptre   [140]
exceed the skills of ordinary men.
That age-old authority of kings
has now come down to you, my son.
So tell me what I need to do to serve you.

NEOPTOLEMUS
Right now perhaps you're eager to inspect
the place here on the shore in which he lives.
You can look through it—there's no need to fear—
that dangerous man has left his cave for now.
When he gets back, stand ready to come out
when I give you the sign. Try to help me.
Provide whatever aid I may require.

CHORUS
My lord, this help you talk about   [150]
has for a long time been my chief concern,
always to keep my eyes alert
above all to what's best for you.

νῦν δέ μοι λέγ', αὐλὰς
ποίας ἔνεδρος ναίει
καὶ χῶρον τίν' ἔχει. τὸ γάρ μοι
μαθεῖν οὐκ ἀποκαίριον,   155
μὴ προσπεσών με λάθῃ ποθέν·
τίς τόπος ἢ τίς ἕδρα; τίν' ἔχει στίβον,
ἔναυλον ἢ θυραῖον;

ΝΕΟΠΤΟΛΕΜΟΣ

οἶκον μὲν ὁρᾷς τόνδ' ἀμφίθυρον
πετρίνης κοίτης.   160

ΧΟΡΟΣ

ποῦ γὰρ ὁ τλήμων αὐτὸς ἄπεστιν;

ΝΕΟΠΤΟΛΕΜΟΣ

δῆλον ἔμοιγ' ὡς φορβῆς χρείᾳ
στίβον ὀγμεύει τῇδε πέλας που.
ταύτην γὰρ ἔχειν βιοτῆς αὐτὸν
λόγος ἐστὶ φύσιν, θηροβολοῦντα   165
πτηνοῖς ἰοῖς στυγερὸν στυγερῶς,
οὐδέ τιν' αὐτῷ
παιῶνα κακῶν ἐπινωμᾶν.

ΧΟΡΟΣ

οἰκτίρω νιν ἔγωγ', ὅπως,
μή του κηδομένου βροτῶν   170
μηδὲ ξύντροφον ὄμμ' ἔχων,
δύστανος, μόνος ἀεί,
νοσεῖ μὲν νόσον ἀγρίαν,
ἀλύει δ' ἐπὶ παντί τῳ
χρείας ἱσταμένῳ. πῶς ποτε πῶς δύσμορος ἀντέχει;   175
ὦ παλάμαι θεῶν,
ὦ δύστανα γένη βροτῶν,
οἷς μὴ μέτριος αἰών.

οὗτος πρωτογόνων ἴσως   180
οἴκων οὐδενὸς ὕστερος,

Tell me some details of this man,
the kind of shelter where he lives,
and where he might be now.
There are things I ought to know,
in case he comes at me somewhere
when I'm not ready for him.
Where has he disappeared?
Is he at home in there,
in that cave, or here outside?

NEOPTOLEMUS
Here's his dwelling with two entrances,
a den carved in the rock.   [160]

CHORUS
                              The man who lives here—
where's the poor wretch gone?

NEOPTOLEMUS
                                    I think that's clear.
He's dragging his foot along some place nearby,
looking for things to eat. I've heard it said
that that's the way he usually lives,
In his sad state it takes what strength he has
to shoot his feathered arrows at his prey,
and no one ever ventures close enough
to help him cure his sick condition.

CHORUS
Well, I pity him for that—
with no human to look after him,   [170]
and no companion's face to see,
he lives a miserable life,
alone, always alone,
infected with a cruel disease,
confused about what he should do
to cope with every pressing need.
How does he bear a fate so grim?
It is the workings of the gods.
What a wretched race of men they are
whose life exceeds due measure.

This man Philoctetes,   [180]
for all we know, is just as good
as any member of the finest clan.

19

Sophocles

πάντων ἄμμορος ἐν βίῳ
κεῖται μοῦνος ἀπ’ ἄλλων,
στικτῶν ἢ λασίων μετὰ
θηρῶν, ἔν τ’ ὀδύναις ὁμοῦ   185
λιμῷ τ’ οἰκτρός, ἀνήκεστα μεριμνήματ’ ἔχων· ὀρεία
    δ’ ἀθυρόστομος
Ἀχὼ τηλεφανὴς πικραῖς
οἰμωγαῖς ὑπακούει.   190

ΝΕΟΠΤΟΛΕΜΟΣ
οὐδὲν τούτων θαυμαστὸν ἐμοί·
θεῖα γάρ, εἴπερ κἀγώ τι φρονῶ,
καὶ τὰ παθήματα κεῖνα πρὸς αὐτὸν
τῆς ὠμόφρονος Χρύσης ἐπέβη,
καὶ νῦν ἃ πονεῖ δίχα κηδεμόνων,   195
οὐκ ἔσθ’ ὡς οὐ θεῶν του μελέτῃ
τοῦ μὴ πρότερον τόνδ’ ἐπὶ Τροίᾳ
τεῖναι τὰ θεῶν ἀμάχητα βέλη,
πρὶν ὅδ’ ἐξήκοι χρόνος, ᾧ λέγεται
χρῆναί σφ’ ὑπὸ τῶνδε δαμῆναι.   200

ΧΟΡΟΣ
εὔστομ’ ἔχε, παῖ.

ΝΕΟΠΤΟΛΕΜΟΣ
            τί τόδε;

ΧΟΡΟΣ
                προυφάνη κτύπος,
φωτὸς σύντροφος ὡς τειρομένου του,
ἤ που τῇδ’ ἢ τῇδε τόπων.
βάλλει βάλλει μ’ ἐτύμα   205
φθογγά του στίβον κατ’ ἀνάγκαν
ἕρποντος, οὐδέ με λάθει
βαρεῖα τηλόθεν αὐδὰ τρυσάνωρ· διάσημα γὰρ θρηνεῖ.
ἀλλ’ ἔχε, τέκνον,

ΝΕΟΠΤΟΛΕΜΟΣ
            λέγ’ ὅ τι.

But here he lies all by himself,
apart from other human beings,
with shaggy goats and spotted deer,
suffering from hunger pangs
and from his painful wound.
It's pitiful—he has to bear
an agony that has no cure,
and, as he cries in bitter pain,
the only answer comes from Echo,
a distant, senseless babble.   [190]

NEOPTOLEMUS

Well, nothing in all this surprises me.
Let me explain just how I understand it.
This man's sufferings come from the gods,
both those afflicting him from savage Chryse
and those he suffers now without a cure.[6]
The gods are planning that Philoctetes
will not aim his bow at Troy and shoot his shafts,
those all-conquering arrows from the gods,
until the time is right, when, people say,
those weapons take the city—that's Troy's fate.   [200]

CHORUS

My lad, be quiet.

NEOPTOLEMUS

                    Why, what's the matter?

CHORUS

I heard a noise—a sound that may have come
from someone in distress. From over there,
I think, or maybe there. Yes, I hear it—
I hear the voice of someone hurt. That's it—
someone forced to crawl along the path.
That heavy groaning of a man in pain,
even from far away, is hard to miss.
The cries are just too clear. Now, my lad,
you should listen . . .

NEOPTOLEMUS

                    To what?

ΧΟΡΟΣ

               φροντίδας νέας.   210
ὡς οὐκ ἔξεδρος, ἀλλ᾽ ἔντοπος ἀνήρ,
οὐ μολπὰν σύριγγος ἔχων,
ὡς ποιμὴν ἀγροβότας, ἀλλ᾽ ἤ που πταίων ὑπ
    ἀνάγκας   215
βοᾷ τηλωπὸν ἰωάν,
ἢ ναὸς ἄξενον αὐγάζων ὅρμον· προβοᾷ τι γὰρ δεινόν.

ΦΙΛΟΚΤΗΤΗΣ

ἰὼ ξένοι,
τίνες ποτ᾽ ἐς γῆν τήνδε κἀκ ποίας πάτρας   220
κατέσχετ᾽ οὔτ᾽ εὔορμον οὔτ᾽ οἰκουμένην;
ποίας ἂν ὑμᾶς πατρίδος ἢ γένους ποτὲ
τύχοιμ᾽ ἂν εἰπών; σχῆμα μὲν γὰρ Ἑλλάδος
στολῆς ὑπάρχει προσφιλεστάτης ἐμοί·
φωνῆς δ᾽ ἀκοῦσαι βούλομαι· καὶ μή μ᾽ ὄκνῳ   225
δείσαντες ἐκπλαγῆτ᾽ ἀπηγριωμένον,
ἀλλ᾽ οἰκτίσαντες ἄνδρα δύστηνον, μόνον,
ἔρημον ὧδε κἄφιλον κακούμενον,
φωνήσατ᾽, εἴπερ ὡς φίλοι προσήκετε.
ἀλλ᾽ ἀνταμείψασθ᾽· οὐ γὰρ εἰκὸς οὔτ᾽ ἐμὲ   230
ὑμῶν ἁμαρτεῖν τοῦτό γ᾽ οὔθ᾽ ὑμᾶς ἐμοῦ.

ΝΕΟΠΤΟΛΕΜΟΣ

ἀλλ᾽, ὦ ξέν᾽, ἴσθι τοῦτο πρῶτον, οὕνεκα
Ἕλληνές ἐσμεν· τοῦτο γὰρ βούλει μαθεῖν.

ΦΙΛΟΚΤΗΤΗΣ

ὦ φίλτατον φώνημα· φεῦ τὸ καὶ λαβεῖν
πρόσφθεγμα τοιοῦδ᾽ ἀνδρὸς ἐν χρόνῳ μακρῷ.   235
τίς σ᾽, ὦ τέκνον, προσέσχε, τίς προσήγαγεν
χρεία; τίς ὁρμή; τίς ἀνέμων ὁ φίλτατος;
γέγωνέ μοι πᾶν τοῦθ᾽, ὅπως εἰδῶ τίς εἶ.

ΝΕΟΠΤΟΛΕΜΟΣ

ἐγὼ γένος μέν εἰμι τῆς περιρρύτου
Σκύρου· πλέω δ᾽ ἐς οἶκον· αὐδῶμαι δὲ παῖς   240
Ἀχιλλέως, Νεοπτόλεμος. οἶσθα δὴ τὸ πᾶν.

CHORUS
                    I've just been thinking.   [210]
This man's not far away—he's close to us,
bringing music home, not like a shepherd
piping his flocks back to some melody,
but screaming as he stumbles.
Perhaps his echoing howls
come from his body's pain
or else he's seen our ship
at its unwelcoming anchorage.
In either case, his cries are dreadful.

[Enter Philoctetes]

PHILOCTETES
                    You there, you strangers,
what country are you from? Why land here,   [220]
put into such a desolate location,
without a decent harbour? If I guessed
your homeland or your family, what answer
would be right? You look as if you're Greeks,
at least from how you're dressed, and that's a sight
that pleases me. But I'd like to hear you speak.
Please don't be afraid of me and run away,
scared because I look like such a savage.
Take pity on a wretched, lonely man,
abandoned without friends, in misery.
If you come as friends, speak up. Answer me.   [230]
It's only right we talk to one another.

NEOPTOLEMUS
Well, stranger, the first thing you should know
is that we're Greeks. That's what you want to hear.

PHILOCTETES
Ah, that language gives me such delight—
to hear such words spoken by a man like this,
after so many years! Tell me, young man,
what made you land here? Something you need?
Some business? Or a friendly wind? Speak up—
tell everything, so I know who you are.

NEOPTOLEMUS
My birthplace is the island Scyros. Right now,
I'm sailing home. I'm Neoptolemus—   [240]
Achilles' son. Now you know everything.

23

Sophocles

ΦΙΛΟΚΤΗΤΗΣ

ὦ φιλτάτου παῖ πατρός, ὦ φίλης χθονός,
ὦ τοῦ γέροντος θρέμμα Λυκομήδους, τίνι
στόλῳ προσέσχες τήνδε γῆν πόθεν πλέων;

ΝΕΟΠΤΟΛΕΜΟΣ

ἐξ Ἰλίου τοι δὴ τανῦν γε ναυστολῶ.   245

ΦΙΛΟΚΤΗΤΗΣ

πῶς εἶπας; οὐ γὰρ δὴ σύ γ᾽ ἦσθα ναυβάτης
ἡμῖν κατ᾽ ἀρχὴν τοῦ πρὸς Ἴλιον στόλου.

ΝΕΟΠΤΟΛΕΜΟΣ

ἦ γὰρ μετέσχες καὶ σὺ τοῦδε τοῦ πόνου;

ΦΙΛΟΚΤΗΤΗΣ

ὦ τέκνον, οὐ γὰρ οἶσθά μ᾽ ὅντιν᾽ εἰσορᾷς;

ΝΕΟΠΤΟΛΕΜΟΣ

πῶς γὰρ κάτοιδ᾽ ὅν γ᾽ εἶδον οὐδεπώποτε;   250

ΦΙΛΟΚΤΗΤΗΣ

οὐδ᾽ ὄνομ᾽ ἄρ᾽ οὐδὲ τῶν ἐμῶν κακῶν κλέος
ᾔσθου ποτ᾽ οὐδέν, οἷς ἐγὼ διωλλύμην;

ΝΕΟΠΤΟΛΕΜΟΣ

ὡς μηδὲν εἰδότ᾽ ἴσθι μ᾽ ὧν ἀνιστορεῖς.

ΦΙΛΟΚΤΗΤΗΣ

ὦ πόλλ᾽ ἐγὼ μοχθηρός, ὦ πικρὸς θεοῖς,   255
οὗ μηδὲ κληδὼν ὧδ᾽ ἔχοντος οἴκαδε
μηδ᾽ Ἑλλάδος γῆς μηδαμοῦ διῆλθέ που.
ἀλλ᾽ οἱ μὲν ἐκβαλόντες ἀνοσίως ἐμὲ
γελῶσι σῖγ᾽ ἔχοντες, ἡ δ᾽ ἐμὴ νόσος
ἀεὶ τέθηλε κἀπὶ μεῖζον ἔρχεται.   260
ὦ τέκνον, ὦ παῖ πατρὸς ἐξ Ἀχιλλέως,
ὅδ᾽ εἴμ᾽ ἐγώ σοι κεῖνος, ὃν κλύεις ἴσως
τῶν Ἡρακλείων ὄντα δεσπότην ὅπλων,

PHILOCTETES
    My lad, son of a man I truly loved,
    and from a land I cherish, you were raised
    by old Lycomedes, your mother's father.
    What business brings you to this island?
    Where are you sailing from?

NEOPTOLEMUS
                Well, if you must know,
    I'm sailing now away from Troy.

PHILOCTETES
                  What's that you say?
    I'm sure you weren't one of those on board
    when our first expedition sailed for Troy.

NEOPTOLEMUS
    Did you take part in that great enterprise?

PHILOCTETES
    My boy, you mean you don't know who I am,
    you have no clue who you are looking at?

NEOPTOLEMUS
    How can I know a man I've never seen?   [250]

PHILOCTETES
    You don't know my name? You've never even heard
    a rumour of my deadly suffering?

NEOPTOLEMUS
    Let me assure you I know none of that—
    I've no idea what you're asking.

PHILOCTETES
    O how truly miserable I must be,
    how bitter to the gods, if not a word,
    not even rumours of my living here,
    have reached my home or any part of Greece.
    Those men who broke god's laws to leave me here
    have hushed it up and laugh, while my disease
    keeps flourishing and getting worse. My boy,
    young lad whose father is Achilles,   [260]
    the man who stands here right in front of you
    is someone you perhaps have heard about
    as master of the arms of Hercules.

ὁ τοῦ Ποίαντος παῖς Φιλοκτήτης, ὃν οἱ
δισσοὶ στρατηγοὶ χὼ Κεφαλλήνων ἄναξ   265
ἔρριψαν αἰσχρῶς ὧδ᾽ ἔρημον, ἀγρίᾳ
νόσῳ καταφθίνοντα, τῆς ἀνδροφθόρου
πληγέντ᾽ ἐχίδνης ἀγρίῳ χαράγματι·
ξὺν ᾗ μ᾽ ἐκεῖνοι, παῖ, προθέντες ἐνθάδε
ᾤχοντ᾽ ἔρημον, ἡνίκ᾽ ἐκ τῆς ποντίας
Χρύσης κατέσχον δεῦρο ναυβάτῃ στόλῳ.   270
τότ᾽ ἄσμενοί μ᾽ ὡς εἶδον ἐκ πολλοῦ σάλου
εὕδοντ᾽ ἐπ᾽ ἀκτῆς ἐν κατηρεφεῖ πέτρᾳ,
λιπόντες ᾤχονθ᾽, οἷα φωτὶ δυσμόρῳ
ῥάκη προθέντες βαιὰ καί τι καὶ βορᾶς
ἐπωφέλημα σμικρόν, οἷ᾽ αὐτοῖς τύχοι.   275
σὺ δή, τέκνον, ποίαν μ᾽ ἀνάστασιν δοκεῖς
αὐτῶν βεβώτων ἐξ ὕπνου στῆναι τότε;
ποῖ᾽ ἐκδακρῦσαι, ποῖ᾽ ἀποιμῶξαι κακά;
ὁρῶντα μὲν ναῦς, ἃς ἔχων ἐναυστόλουν,
πάσας βεβώσας, ἄνδρα δ᾽ οὐδέν᾽ ἔντοπον,   280
οὐχ ὅστις ἀρκέσειεν οὐδ᾽ ὅστις νόσου
κάμνοντι συλλάβοιτο· πάντα δὲ σκοπῶν
ηὕρισκον οὐδὲν πλὴν ἀνιᾶσθαι παρόν,
τούτου δὲ πολλὴν εὐμάρειαν, ὦ τέκνον.
ὁ μὲν χρόνος δὴ διὰ χρόνου προύβαινέ μοι,   285
κᾆδεῖ τι βαιᾷ τῇδ᾽ ὑπὸ στέγῃ μόνον
διακονεῖσθαι. γαστρὶ μὲν τὰ σύμφορα
τόξον τόδ᾽ ἐξηύρισκε, τὰς ὑποπτέρους
βάλλον πελείας· πρὸς δὲ τοῦθ᾽, ὅ μοι βάλοι
νευροσπαδὴς ἄτρακτος, αὐτὸς ἂν τάλας   290
εἰλυόμην, δύστηνον ἐξέλκων πόδα,
πρὸς τοῦτ᾽ ἄν· εἴ τ᾽ ἔδει τι καὶ ποτὸν λαβεῖν,
καί που πάγου χυθέντος, οἷα χείματι,
ξύλον τι θραῦσαι, ταῦτ᾽ ἂν ἐξέρπων τάλας
ἐμηχανώμην· εἶτα πῦρ ἂν οὐ παρῆν,   295
ἀλλ᾽ ἐν πέτροισι πέτρον ἐκτρίβων μόλις
ἔφην᾽ ἄφαντον φῶς, ὃ καὶ σῴζει μ᾽ ἀεί.

Yes, I am Poeas' son, Philoctetes,
the man those two commanders of the army
and that Cephallenian king, Odysseus,
so disgracefully threw out, deserted here,
while I was suffering this cruel disease.7
I was bitten by a savage deadly snake.
Our fleet had sailed from Chryse by the sea.   [270]
It landed here. Then, my boy, they left me
with this infection as my sole companion.
Yes, they left me here alone. Once they saw
my storms of pain had passed and I was sleeping,
they were so happy to abandon me
under an overhanging rock, here onshore,
setting out some rags, some scraps of food,
a pittance—enough to please a beggar.
I hope they get the treatment they gave me!
My boy, can you imagine how I felt
after my sleep that day, when I awoke,
when I got up to find they'd disappeared?
How I wept, how I cried out in distress,
when I saw the ships on which I'd sailed
had all gone off, with no one else around,   [280]
no one to help, no one to soothe the ache
of my disease? I looked everywhere,
but all I found around me was my pain.
Of that, my lad, I had more than my share.
Well, time went by for me, month after month,
alone in this small shelter. I was forced
to look to my own needs all by myself.
This bow gave me the food my stomach craved,
by shooting birds as they passed overhead.
Each time an arrow flew out from this string   [290]
and struck, I'd go crawling after it, in pain,
dragging this wretched foot behind me.
In winter, when I needed to fetch water,
often there was frost—at that time of year
it's not uncommon—and I'd have to break
some firewood. I'd drag myself outside,
in agony, and get it. Then, at times,
I had no fire. But by rubbing stones
I finally produced the hidden spark
which keeps me going day by day. In fact,

Sophocles

οἰκουμένη γὰρ οὖν στέγη πυρὸς μέτα
πάντ᾽ ἐκπορίζει πλὴν τὸ μὴ νοσεῖν ἐμέ.
φέρ᾽, ὦ τέκνον, νῦν καὶ τὸ τῆς νήσου μάθῃς.   300
ταύτῃ πελάζει ναυβάτης οὐδεὶς ἑκών·
οὐ γάρ τις ὅρμος ἔστιν οὐδ᾽ ὅποι πλέων
ἐξεμπολήσει κέρδος ἢ ξενώσεται.
οὐκ ἐνθάδ᾽ οἱ πλοῖ τοῖσι σώφροσιν βροτῶν.
τάχ᾽ οὖν τις ἄκων ἔσχε· πολλὰ γὰρ τάδε   305
ἐν τῷ μακρῷ γένοιτ᾽ ἂν ἀνθρώπων χρόνῳ·
οὗτοί μ᾽, ὅταν μόλωσιν, ὦ τέκνον, λόγοις
ἐλεοῦσι μέν, καί πού τι καὶ βορᾶς μέρος
προσέδοσαν οἰκτίραντες ἤ τινα στολήν·
ἐκεῖνο δ᾽ οὐδείς, ἡνίκ᾽ ἂν μνησθῶ, θέλει,   310
σῶσαί μ᾽ ἐς οἴκους, ἀλλ᾽ ἀπόλλυμαι τάλας
ἔτος τόδ᾽ ἤδη δέκατον ἐν λιμῷ τε καὶ
κακοῖσι βόσκων τὴν ἀδηφάγον νόσον.
τοιαῦτ᾽ Ἀτρεῖδαί μ᾽ ἥ τ᾽ Ὀδυσσέως βία,
ὦ παῖ, δεδράκασ᾽, οἷ᾽ Ὀλύμπιοι θεοὶ   315
δοῖέν ποτ᾽ αὐτοῖς ἀντίποιν᾽ ἐμοῦ παθεῖν.

ΧΟΡΟΣ
ἔοικα κἀγὼ τοῖς ἀφιγμένοις ἴσα
ξένοις ἐποικτίρειν σε, Ποίαντος τέκνον.

ΝΕΟΠΤΟΛΕΜΟΣ
ἐγὼ δὲ καὐτὸς τοῖσδε μάρτυς ἐν λόγοις,
ὡς εἴσ᾽ ἀληθεῖς οἶδα, συντυχὼν κακῶν   320
ἀνδρῶν Ἀτρειδῶν τῆς τ᾽ Ὀδυσσέως βίας.

ΦΙΛΟΚΤΗΤΗΣ
ἦ γάρ τι καὶ σὺ τοῖς πανωλέθροις ἔχεις
ἔγκλημ᾽ Ἀτρείδαις, ὥστε θυμοῦσθαι παθών;

ΝΕΟΠΤΟΛΕΜΟΣ
θυμὸν γένοιτο χειρὶ πληρῶσαί ποτε,
ἵν᾽ αἱ Μυκῆναι γνοῖεν ἡ Σπάρτη θ᾽ ὅτι   325
χἡ Σκῦρος ἀνδρῶν ἀλκίμων μήτηρ ἔφυ.

28

living here under this roof and with my fire
I have all I need, except, of course,
relief from my disease. You see, my lad, [300]
you should know some facts about this island.
No sailor ever comes too near this place—
not if he can help it. There's no moorage
or any port where he can buy and sell
to make a profit or find a welcome host.
So men with any sense don't travel here.
If someone ever came unwillingly—
such things do happen often over time
in the full span of one's life—well then,
when they arrived, my boy, they'd talk to me,
speak a few sympathetic words, and then,
from pity, add some food or clothing.
But there's one thing no one would ever do, [310]
once I suggested it—take me safely home.
This is the tenth year of my misery,
wasting away in hunger and distress,
eaten up by this gluttonous disease.
This is the work of those sons of Atreus
and Odysseus, that brutal man. They did this.
May the Olympian gods give them someday
full retribution for my agonies!

CHORUS

Son of Poeas, I pity you, as well—
just like those visitors you had before.

NEOPTOLEMUS

I, too, can testify to what you say.
You speak the truth. For I've experienced [320]
how bad the sons of Atreus can be,
and Odysseus' brutality as well.

PHILOCTETES

What's that? You mean you, too, have complaints
against those cursed sons of Atreus—
something they did to you to make you angry?

NEOPTOLEMUS

I wish one day my hand could vent my rage,
so then they'd learn in Sparta and Mycenae,
that Scyros is the mother of brave men.[8]

29

Sophocles

ΦΙΛΟΚΤΗΤΗΣ

εὖ γ᾽, ὦ τέκνον· τίνος γὰρ ὦδε τὸν μέγαν
χόλον κατ᾽ αὐτῶν ἐγκαλῶν ἐλήλυθας;

ΝΕΟΠΤΟΛΕΜΟΣ

ὦ παῖ Ποίαντος, ἐξερῶ, μόλις δ᾽ ἐρῶ,
ἄγωγ᾽ ὑπ᾽ αὐτῶν ἐξελωβήθην μολών.   330
ἐπεὶ γὰρ ἔσχε μοῖρ᾽ Ἀχιλλέα θανεῖν,

ΦΙΛΟΚΤΗΤΗΣ

οἴμοι· φράσῃς μοι μὴ πέρα, πρὶν ἂν μάθω
πρῶτον τόδ᾽, ἦ τέθνηχ᾽ ὁ Πηλέως γόνος;

ΝΕΟΠΤΟΛΕΜΟΣ

τέθνηκεν, ἀνδρὸς οὐδενός, θεοῦ δ᾽ ὕπο,
τοξευτός, ὡς λέγουσιν, ἐκ Φοίβου δαμείς.   335

ΦΙΛΟΚΤΗΤΗΣ

ἀλλ᾽ εὐγενὴς μὲν ὁ κτανών τε χὠ θανών·
ἀμηχανῶ δὲ πότερον, ὦ τέκνον, τὸ σὸν
πάθημ᾽ ἐλέγχω πρῶτον ἢ κεῖνον στένω.

ΝΕΟΠΤΟΛΕΜΟΣ

οἶμαι μὲν ἀρκεῖν σοί γε καὶ τὰ σ᾽, ὦ τάλας,
ἀλγήμαθ᾽, ὥστε μὴ τὰ τῶν πέλας στένειν.   340

ΦΙΛΟΚΤΗΤΗΣ

ὀρθῶς ἔλεξας· τοιγαροῦν τὸ σὸν φράσον
αὖθις πάλιν μοι πρᾶγμ᾽, ὅτῳ σ᾽ ἐνύβρισαν.

ΝΕΟΠΤΟΛΕΜΟΣ

ἦλθόν με νηὶ ποικιλοστόλῳ μέτα
δῖός τ᾽ Ὀδυσσεὺς χὠ τροφεὺς τοὐμοῦ πατρός,
λέγοντες, εἴτ᾽ ἀληθὲς εἴτ᾽ ἄρ᾽ οὖν μάτην,   345
ὡς οὐ θέμις γίγνοιτ᾽, ἐπεὶ κατέφθιτο
πατὴρ ἐμός, τὰ πέργαμ᾽ ἄλλον ἤ μ᾽ ἑλεῖν.

PHILOCTETES

    Good for you, my lad. But what's your reason?
    Why are you so angry? What's the grudge
    you have against them?

NEOPTOLEMUS

                I'll tell you, son of Poeas,
    but it's hard to say what I went through   [330]
    on their account when I arrived at Troy.
    When fate declared Achilles had to die . . .

PHILOCTETES *[interrupting]*

    What's that? Stop there. Answer this question first—
    is Achilles, son of Peleus, dead?

NEOPTOLEMUS

                      He is.
    But no mortal killed him. It was a god.
    Phoebus Apollo brought him down, they say,
    with an arrow shot.

PHILOCTETES

                Both noble beings,
    the killer and the killed. Now I'm not sure,
    my boy, what I should do next—question you
    about your suffering or mourn Achilles.

NEOPTOLEMUS

    Your own afflictions are enough for you,
    I think. You unhappy man, you don't need
    to mourn the next man's troubles.

PHILOCTETES

                    You're right.
    So tell me once again what you went through,
    how those men harmed you.

NEOPTOLEMUS

             They came to get me
    in a fancy, decorated ship—Phoenix,
    who raised my father, and lord Odysseus.
    They said—I don't know if it's true or not—
    that since my father had been killed,
    destiny decreed that no one except me
    could seize those towers in Troy. Well, my friend,

ταῦτ᾽, ὦ ξέν᾽, οὕτως ἐννέποντες οὐ πολὺν
χρόνον μ᾽ ἐπέσχον μή με ναυστολεῖν ταχύ,
μάλιστα μὲν δὴ τοῦ θανόντος ἱμέρῳ,   350
ὅπως ἴδοιμ᾽ ἄθαπτον· οὐ γὰρ εἰδόμην·
ἔπειτα μέντοι χὠ λόγος καλὸς προσῆν,
εἰ τἀπὶ Τροίᾳ πέργαμ᾽ αἱρήσοιμ᾽ ἰών.
ἦν δ᾽ ἦμαρ ἤδη δεύτερον πλέοντί μοι,
κἀγὼ πικρὸν Σίγειον οὐρίῳ πλάτῃ   355
κατηγόμην· καί μ᾽ εὐθὺς ἐν κύκλῳ στρατὸς
ἐκβάντα πᾶς ἠσπάζετ᾽, ὀμνύντες βλέπειν
τὸν οὐκέτ᾽ ὄντα ζῶντ᾽ Ἀχιλλέα πάλιν.
κεῖνος μὲν οὖν ἔκειτ᾽· ἐγὼ δ᾽ ὁ δύσμορος
ἐπεὶ ᾽δάκρυσα κεῖνον, οὐ μακρῷ χρόνῳ   360
ἐλθὼν Ἀτρείδας πρὸς φίλους, ὡς εἰκὸς ἦν,
τά θ᾽ ὅπλ᾽ ἀπήτουν τοῦ πατρὸς τά τ᾽ ἄλλ᾽ ὅσ᾽ ἦν.
οἱ δ᾽ εἶπον, οἴμοι, τλημονέστατον λόγον·
'ὦ σπέρμ᾽ Ἀχιλλέως, τἄλλα μὲν πάρεστί σοι
πατρῷ᾽ ἑλέσθαι, τῶν δ᾽ ὅπλων κείνων ἀνὴρ   365
ἄλλος κρατύνει νῦν, ὁ Λαέρτου γόνος.'
κἀγὼ δακρύσας εὐθὺς ἐξανίσταμαι
ὀργῇ βαρείᾳ, καὶ καταλγήσας λέγω·
'ὦ σχέτλι᾽, ἦ ᾽τολμήσατ᾽ ἀντ᾽ ἐμοῦ τινι
δοῦναι τὰ τεύχη τἀμά, πρὶν μαθεῖν ἐμοῦ;'   370
ὁ δ᾽ εἶπ᾽ Ὀδυσσεύς, πλησίον γὰρ ὢν κυρεῖ,
'ναί, παῖ, δεδώκασ᾽ ἐνδίκως οὗτοι τάδε·
ἐγὼ γὰρ αὔτ᾽ ἔσωσα κἀκεῖνον παρών.'
κἀγὼ χολωθεὶς εὐθὺς ἤρασσον κακοῖς
τοῖς πᾶσιν, οὐδὲν ἐνδεὲς ποιούμενος,   375
εἰ τἀμὰ κεῖνος ὅπλ᾽ ἀφαιρήσοιτό με.
ὁ δ᾽ ἐνθάδ᾽ ἥκων, καίπερ οὐ δύσοργος ὤν,
δηχθεὶς πρὸς ἀξήκουσεν ὧδ᾽ ἠμείψατο·
'οὐκ ἦσθ᾽ ἵν᾽ ἡμεῖς, ἀλλ᾽ ἀπῆσθ᾽ ἵν᾽ οὔ σ᾽ ἔδει·
καὶ ταῦτ᾽, ἐπειδὴ καὶ λέγεις θρασυστομῶν,   380
οὐ μήποτ᾽ ἐς τὴν Σκῦρον ἐκπλεύσῃς ἔχων.'

once they'd said that, they gave me little time
before we left. We sailed there at top speed,
mainly because I had a great desire [350]
to see my father's corpse before the burial,
since I'd never seen him. In addition,
what they said to me was truly wonderful—
if I went back with them, I'd capture Troy.
Well, we rowed and had a favorable wind,
so on my voyage by the second day
we had reached Sigeum, that bitter place.9
Then, when I disembarked, all the army
at once came crowding round to welcome me,
swearing they could see the dead Achilles
alive again. But he just lay there dead.
In my grief I wept for him. Soon after that, [360]
I went to Atreus' sons, as friends of mine,
or so I thought, to claim my father's arms
and all the rest of what belonged to him.
They gave me the most shameless of replies—
"Seed of Achilles, you may take away
all your father's things except his weapons.
Another man is master of them now,
Laertes' son, Odysseus." I jumped up—
my anger was immediate and intense—
tears were in my eyes. Full of bitterness,
I yelled at them, "You miserable men,
have you two dared award my weapons
to another man rather than to me [370]
without even bothering to tell me?"
Then Odysseus spoke up—it so happened
he was there nearby—"Yes, boy, they did.
And rightly, too, because I rescued them.
I was there to save their master's body."
In my rage I began to heap on him
every insult I could think of, all at once.
If he meant to steal those weapons from me,
then there was nothing I was holding back.
Hurt by my abuse, though not enraged,
Odysseus said, "You've not been where we have—
you weren't around when we all needed you.
And now, since you cannot speak politely, [380]
you'll never sail to Scyros with those arms."

33

Sophocles

τοιαῦτ᾽ ἀκούσας κἀξονειδισθεὶς κακὰ
πλέω πρὸς οἴκους, τῶν ἐμῶν τητώμενος
πρὸς τοῦ κακίστου κἀκ κακῶν Ὀδυσσέως.
κοὐκ αἰτιῶμαι κεῖνον ὡς τοὺς ἐν τέλει·   385
πόλις γάρ ἐστι πᾶσα τῶν ἡγουμένων
στρατός τε σύμπας· οἱ δ᾽ ἀκοσμοῦντες βροτῶν
διδασκάλων λόγοισι γίγνονται κακοί.
λόγος λέλεκται πᾶς· ὁ δ᾽ Ἀτρείδας στυγῶν
ἐμοί θ᾽ ὁμοίως καὶ θεοῖς εἴη φίλος.   390

ΧΟΡΟΣ

ὀρεστέρα παμβῶτι Γᾶ, μᾶτερ αὐτοῦ Διός,
ἃ τὸν μέγαν Πακτωλὸν εὔχρυσον νέμεις,
σὲ κἀκεῖ, μᾶτερ πότνι᾽, ἐπηυδώμαν,   395
ὅτ᾽ ἐς τόνδ᾽ Ἀτρειδᾶν ὕβρις πᾶσ᾽ ἐχώρει,
ὅτε τὰ πάτρια τεύχεα παρεδίδοσαν,
ἰὼ μάκαιρα ταυροκτόνων   400
λεόντων ἔφεδρε, τῷ Λαρτίου
σέβας ὑπέρτατον.

ΦΙΛΟΚΤΗΤΗΣ

ἔχοντες, ὡς ἔοικε, σύμβολον σαφὲς
λύπης πρὸς ἡμᾶς, ὦ ξένοι, πεπλεύκατε,
καί μοι προσᾴδεθ᾽ ὥστε γιγνώσκειν ὅτι   405
ταῦτ᾽ ἐξ Ἀτρειδῶν ἔργα κἀξ Ὀδυσσέως.
ἔξοιδα γάρ νιν παντὸς ἂν λόγου κακοῦ
γλώσσῃ θιγόντα καὶ πανουργίας, ἀφ᾽ ἧς
μηδὲν δίκαιον ἐς τέλος μέλλοι ποεῖν.
ἀλλ᾽ οὔ τι τοῦτο θαῦμ᾽ ἔμοιγ᾽, ἀλλ᾽ εἰ παρὼν   410
Αἴας ὁ μείζων ταῦθ᾽ ὁρῶν ἠνείχετο.

34

After hearing such rebukes and insults,
I'm sailing home without my property,
thanks to that low-born criminal Odysseus.
But I don't lay the blame so much on him
as on those in command. For any city
depends completely on those in control,
and so must all the army. And when people
grow unruly, it's what their teachers say
that makes them so corrupt. That's my story,
all I have to tell. If there's anyone
who hates those sons of Atreus, I hope
the gods will cherish him the way I do.   [390]

CHORUS
    All-nourishing mountain mother Earth,
    mother of Zeus himself,
    you who live and rule
    in great Pactolus, rich in gold,
    most dread and sacred mother,
    over there I called on you,
    in Troy, when sons of Atreus
    heaped all their insults on this man,
    while they were handing over
    his father's armour to Odysseus,
    paying highest honours to that man—
    such awe-inspiring things.
    Hail, blessed goddess, as you sit   [400]
    on your splendid decorated throne,
    where carved-out lions slaughter bulls.[10]

PHILOCTETES
    You've sailed here carrying your grief,
    pain like my own, a certain guarantee.
    You and your story harmonize with mine,
    so I can recognize how those men act,
    the sons of Atreus and that Odysseus,
    a man who, I know well, would set his tongue
    to every evil lie or debased act
    to get the unjust end he's looking for.
    No, what you've said does not surprise me,   [410]
    though I do wonder how great Ajax,
    if he was there, could bear to witness it.

35

Sophocles

ΝΕΟΠΤΟΛΕΜΟΣ

οὐκ ἦν ἔτι ζῶν, ὦ ξέν'· οὐ γὰρ ἄν ποτε
ζῶντός γ' ἐκείνου ταῦτ' ἐσυλήθην ἐγώ.

ΦΙΛΟΚΤΗΤΗΣ

πῶς εἶπας; ἀλλ' ἦ χοῦτος οἴχεται θανών;

ΝΕΟΠΤΟΛΕΜΟΣ

ὡς μηκέτ' ὄντα κεῖνον ἐν φάει νόει.   415

ΦΙΛΟΚΤΗΤΗΣ

οἴμοι τάλας. ἀλλ' οὐχ ὁ Τυδέως γόνος
οὐδ' οὑμπολητὸς Σισύφου Λαερτίῳ,
οὐ μὴ θάνωσι· τούσδε γὰρ μὴ ζῆν ἔδει.

ΝΕΟΠΤΟΛΕΜΟΣ

οὐ δῆτ'· ἐπίστω τοῦτό γ'· ἀλλὰ καὶ μέγα
θάλλοντές εἰσι νῦν ἐν Ἀργείων στρατῷ.   420

ΦΙΛΟΚΤΗΤΗΣ

τί δ'; οὐ παλαιὸς κἀγαθὸς φίλος τ' ἐμός,
Νέστωρ ὁ Πύλιος, ἔστιν; οὗτος γὰρ τά γε
κείνων κάκ' ἐξήρυκε, βουλεύων σοφά.

ΝΕΟΠΤΟΛΕΜΟΣ

κεῖνός γε πράσσει νῦν κακῶς, ἐπεὶ θανὼν
Ἀντίλοχος αὐτῷ φροῦδος, ὃς παρῆν, γόνος.   425

ΦΙΛΟΚΤΗΤΗΣ

οἴμοι, δύ' αὖ τώδ' ἄνδρ' ἔλεξας, οἶν ἐγὼ
ἥκιστ' ἂν ἠθέλησ' ὀλωλότοιν κλύειν.
φεῦ φεῦ· τί δῆτα δεῖ σκοπεῖν, ὅθ' οἴδε μὲν
τεθνᾶσ', Ὀδυσσεὺς δ' ἔστιν αὖ κἀνταῦθ' ἵνα
χρῆν ἀντὶ τούτων αὐτὸν αὐδᾶσθαι νεκρόν;   430

ΝΕΟΠΤΟΛΕΜΟΣ

σοφὸς παλαιστὴς κεῖνος· ἀλλὰ χαὶ σοφαὶ
γνῶμαι, Φιλοκτῆτ', ἐμποδίζονται θαμά.

36

NEOPTOLEMUS
> My friend, Ajax was no longer living—
> had he been alive, they'd not have robbed me.

PHILOCTETES
> What's that you say? Did death get Ajax, too?

NEOPTOLEMUS
> He's dead and gone. Imagine Ajax
> no longer standing in the sunlight.

PHILOCTETES
> No, no. It's dreadful. But Diomedes,
> son of Tydeus, and that Odysseus,
> son of Sisyphus (so people say), sold
> to Laertes still in his mother's womb,
> they'll not die, for they don't deserve to live.[11]

NEOPTOLEMUS
> No they won't. That's something you can count on.
> In fact, right now within the Argive army   [420]
> those two are really thriving.

PHILOCTETES
>   And Nestor?
> What about that fine old friend of mine
> from Pylos? Is he alive? He's the one
> who with his prudent counsel often checked
> the nasty things that those two men would do.

NEOPTOLEMUS
> Right now he's not doing well. That son of his,
> Antilochus, who stood by him, is dead.

PHILOCTETES
> That's more bad news. Those two men you mention—
> I really didn't want to hear they'd died.
> God knows what we should look for in this world,
> when such men perish and Odysseus lives,
> and at a time when we should hear the news
> that he was dead instead of those two men.   [430]

NEOPTOLEMUS
> He's a slippery wrestler, Philoctetes,
> but even clever schemes are often checked.

37

Sophocles

ΦΙΛΟΚΤΗΤΗΣ

φέρ᾽ εἰπὲ πρὸς θεῶν, ποῦ γὰρ ἦν ἐνταῦθά σοι
Πάτροκλος, ὃς σοῦ πατρὸς ἦν τὰ φίλτατα;

ΝΕΟΠΤΟΛΕΜΟΣ

χοῦτος τεθνηκὼς ἦν· λόγῳ δέ σ᾽ ἐν βραχεῖ   435
τοῦτ᾽ ἐκδιδάξω· πόλεμος οὐδέν᾽ ἄνδρ᾽ ἑκὼν
αἱρεῖ πονηρόν, ἀλλὰ τοὺς χρηστοὺς ἀεί.

ΦΙΛΟΚΤΗΤΗΣ

ξυμμαρτυρῶ σοι· καὶ κατ᾽ αὐτὸ τοῦτό γε
ἀναξίου μὲν φωτὸς ἐξερήσομαι,
γλώσσῃ δὲ δεινοῦ καὶ σοφοῦ, τί νῦν κυρεῖ.   440

ΝΕΟΠΤΟΛΕΜΟΣ

ποίου δὲ τούτου πλήν γ᾽ Ὀδυσσέως ἐρεῖς;

ΦΙΛΟΚΤΗΤΗΣ

οὐ τοῦτον εἶπον, ἀλλὰ Θερσίτης τις ἦν,
ὃς οὐκ ἂν εἵλετ᾽ εἰσάπαξ εἰπεῖν, ὅπου
μηδεὶς ἐῴη· τοῦτον οἶσθ᾽ εἰ ζῶν κυρεῖ;

ΝΕΟΠΤΟΛΕΜΟΣ

οὐκ εἶδον αὐτόν, ᾐσθόμην δ᾽ ἔτ᾽ ὄντα νιν.   445

ΦΙΛΟΚΤΗΤΗΣ

ἔμελλ᾽· ἐπεὶ οὐδέν πω κακόν γ᾽ ἀπώλετο,
ἀλλ᾽ εὖ περιστέλλουσιν αὐτὰ δαίμονες,
καί πως τὰ μὲν πανοῦργα καὶ παλιντριβῆ
χαίρουσ᾽ ἀναστρέφοντες ἐξ Ἅιδου, τὰ δὲ
δίκαια καὶ τὰ χρήστ᾽ ἀποστέλλουσ᾽ ἀεί.   450
ποῦ χρὴ τίθεσθαι ταῦτα, ποῦ δ᾽ αἰνεῖν, ὅταν
τὰ θεῖ᾽ ἐπαινῶν τοὺς θεοὺς εὕρω κακούς;

PHILOCTETES

    Now, for the gods' sake, what of Patroclus?
    On that occasion where was he? Tell me.
    Your father loved him more than anyone.

NEOPTOLEMUS

    He was also dead. I can tell you why
    in one brief saying—given the choice,
    war takes no evil men. It always wants
    to seize the good ones.

PHILOCTETES

               There I agree with you.
    With that in mind, let me ask you this—
    what about that worthless man who was so glib,
    so daring with his tongue and yet so smart?   [440]

NEOPTOLEMUS

    Surely that can only mean Odysseus?

PHILOCTETES

    No, I don't mean him. There was a man there
    called Thersites, who never was content
    to speak up only once, although no one
    ever granted him the right to speak at all.
    Do you know if that fellow's still alive?[12]

NEOPTOLEMUS

    I haven't seen him. But from what I've heard
    the man still lives.

PHILOCTETES

              Of course, he does.
    No evil people ever get destroyed.
    The gods are careful to look out for them.
    Somehow with all those stubborn criminals
    they like to turn them back from Hades,
    while always sending good and righteous men   [450]
    down to their deaths. How can I sort that out?
    How can I praise the gods? When I give thanks
    for how the world's divinely organized,
    I find the gods themselves disgraceful.

Sophocles

ΝΕΟΠΤΟΛΕΜΟΣ
ἐγὼ μέν, ὦ γένεθλον Οἰταίου πατρός,
τὸ λοιπὸν ἤδη τηλόθεν τό τ᾽ Ἴλιον
καὶ τοὺς Ἀτρείδας εἰσορῶν φυλάξομαι·   455
ὅπου δ᾽ ὁ χείρων τἀγαθοῦ μεῖζον σθένει
κἀποφθίνει τὰ χρηστὰ χὠ δειλὸς κρατεῖ,
τούτους ἐγὼ τοὺς ἄνδρας οὐ στέρξω ποτέ·
ἀλλ᾽ ἡ πετραία Σκῦρος ἐξαρκοῦσά μοι
ἔσται τὸ λοιπόν, ὥστε τέρπεσθαι δόμῳ.   460
νῦν δ᾽ εἶμι πρὸς ναῦν· καὶ σύ, Ποίαντος τέκνον,
χαῖρ᾽ ὡς μέγιστα, χαῖρε· καί σε δαίμονες
νόσου μεταστήσειαν, ὡς αὐτὸς θέλεις.
ἡμεῖς δ᾽ ἴωμεν, ὡς ὁπηνίκ᾽ ἂν θεὸς
πλοῦν ἡμῖν εἴκῃ, τηνικαῦθ᾽ ὁρμώμεθα.   465

ΦΙΛΟΚΤΗΤΗΣ
ἤδη, τέκνον, στέλλεσθε;

ΝΕΟΠΤΟΛΕΜΟΣ
                          καιρὸς γὰρ καλεῖ
πλοῦν μὴ ᾽ξ ἀπόπτου μᾶλλον ἢ ᾽γγύθεν σκοπεῖν.

ΦΙΛΟΚΤΗΤΗΣ
πρός νύν σε πατρὸς πρός τε μητρός, ὦ τέκνον,
πρός τ᾽ εἴ τί σοι κατ᾽ οἶκόν ἐστι προσφιλές,
ἱκέτης ἱκνοῦμαι, μὴ λίπῃς μ᾽ οὕτω μόνον,   470
ἔρημον ἐν κακοῖσι τοῖσδ᾽ οἵοις ὁρᾷς
ὅσοισί τ᾽ ἐξήκουσας ἐνναίοντά με·
ἀλλ᾽ ἐν παρέργῳ θοῦ με. δυσχέρεια μέν,
ἔξοιδα, πολλὴ τοῦδε τοῦ φορήματος·
ὅμως δὲ τλῆθι· τοῖσι γενναίοισί τοι   475
τό τ᾽ αἰσχρὸν ἐχθρὸν καὶ τὸ χρηστὸν εὐκλεές.
σοὶ δ᾽ ἐκλιπόντι τοῦτ᾽ ὄνειδος οὐ καλόν,
δράσαντι δ᾽, ὦ παῖ, πλεῖστον εὐκλείας γέρας,
ἐὰν μόλω ᾽γὼ ζῶν πρὸς Οὐταίαν χθόνα.

40

NEOPTOLEMUS

    Well, Philoctetes, you son of Poeas
    from Oetea, in future I'll be careful—
    I'll keep watching what's going on at Troy
    but from a distance, and I'll do the same
    with those two sons of Atreus. Where I see
    lesser men in someone's camp prevail
    over their betters, so good men waste away,
    while cowards rule, among such groups as these
    I'll never make my friends. No, Scyros' rock
    will be enough for me from this day on.
    I'll be a happy man in my own home.   [460]
    Now, I'll get back to my ship. Farewell,
    Philoctetes—as best you can fare well.
    I pray the gods will rid you of disease,
    in answer to your wishes. We must be off,
    ready to sail out when the god permits.

PHILOCTETES

    My lad, are you setting off already?

NEOPTOLEMUS

    Yes. Our opportunities are telling us
    to wait close to our ship for a good wind
    and not move far away.

PHILOCTETES

                   And now, my boy,
    by your father, by your mother, by all
    the things you love in your own home,
    I come to you a suppliant—don't leave me,   [470]
    not alone like this, living helplessly
    in such distress. You see what this is like.
    You've heard how much I suffer. Think of me
    as something incidental. Yes, I know
    you have a great disgust for such a load.
    But even so, bear with it. Noble minds
    find unkind deeds disgraceful and commend
    good acts, and so if you turn down this plea,
    what people say about you won't be good.
    But my boy, if you do help, you'll win
    the greatest tribute given to honour,
    if I can reach Oeta's land alive.

41

Sophocles

ἴθ'· ἡμέρας τοι μόχθος οὐχ ὅλης μιᾶς. 480
τόλμησον. ἐμβαλοῦ μ' ὅπῃ θέλεις ἄγων,
εἰς ἀντλίαν, εἰς πρῷραν, εἰς πρύμνην, ὅποι
ἥκιστα μέλλω τοὺς ξυνόντας ἀλγυνεῖν.
νεῦσον, πρὸς αὐτοῦ Ζηνὸς ἱκεσίου, τέκνον,
πείσθητι· προσπίτνω σε γόνασι, καίπερ ὢν 485
ἀκράτωρ ὁ τλήμων, χωλός. ἀλλὰ μή μ' ἀφῇς
ἔρημον οὕτω χωρὶς ἀνθρώπων στίβου,
ἀλλ' ἢ πρὸς οἶκον τὸν σὸν ἔκσωσόν μ' ἄγων
ἢ πρὸς τὰ Χαλκώδοντος Εὐβοίας σταθμά·
κἀκεῖθεν οὔ μοι μακρὸς εἰς Οἴτην στόλος 490
Τραχινίαν τε δειράδ' ἠδ' ἐς εὔροον
Σπερχειὸν ἔσται· πατρί μ' ὡς δείξῃς φίλῳ,
ὃν δὴ παλαιὸν ἐξ ὅτου δέδοικ' ἐγὼ
μή μοι βεβήκῃ. πολλὰ γὰρ τοῖς ἱγμένοις
ἔστελλον αὐτὸν ἱκεσίους πέμπων λιτάς, 495
αὐτόστολον πέμψαντά μ' ἐκσῶσαι δόμους.
ἀλλ' ἢ τέθνηκεν ἢ τὰ τῶν διακόνων,
ὡς εἰκός, οἶμαι, τοὐμὸν ἐν σμικρῷ μέρος
ποιούμενοι τὸν οἴκαδ' ἤπειγον στόλον.
νῦν δ', εἰς σὲ γὰρ πομπόν τε καὐτὸν ἄγγελον 500
ἥκω, σὺ σῶσον, σύ μ' ἐλέησον, εἰσορῶν
ὡς πάντα δεινὰ κἀπικινδύνως βροτοῖς
κεῖται παθεῖν μὲν εὖ, παθεῖν δὲ θάτερα.
χρὴ δ' ἐκτὸς ὄντα πημάτων τὰ δείν' ὁρᾶν,
χὤταν τις εὖ ζῇ, τηνικαῦτα τὸν βίον 505
σκοπεῖν μάλιστα, μὴ διαφθαρεὶς λάθῃ.

ΧΟΡΟΣ

οἴκτιρ', ἄναξ· πολλῶν ἔλεξεν δυσοίστων πόνων
ἆθλ', οἷα μηδεὶς τῶν ἐμῶν τύχοι φίλων.

42

Come, not even one full day of trouble. [480]
Take the chance. Let me aboard, and set me
any place you wish—in the hold, the bow,
the stern—wherever I will least offend
the others in the ship. Give your consent,
my boy! By Zeus himself, god of suppliants,
let me convince you! I'm on my knees
in front of you, although I'm weak and ill,
a cripple. Don't leave me all alone like this,
so far from any routes men travel on.
No. Take me safely to your home, or else
to Euboea, where Chalcodon lives.
From there it's no long trip for me to reach [490]
Oeta, the Trachianian heights,
and the fair-flowing Spercheius river,
so you can show me off to my dear father,
although for some time now I've been afraid
he's gone from me. I've often summoned him,
sending urgent prayers with those who've come here,
for him to send a ship to rescue me
and take me home. But either he is dead,
or, what I think more likely, those I asked,
thinking my affairs a trivial thing,
hurried to complete their voyage home.
But now in you I've come across a man [500]
who can carry me and be my messenger.
Have mercy, and rescue me! Bear in mind
how everything for human beings is strange
and so precarious—things can go well,
then change into their opposite. A man
who stays away from harm has to watch out
for dreadful things, and when a man succeeds,
then he must really look at how he lives,
in case he is destroyed without a warning.

CHORUS
O my king, have pity.
He's spoken of his struggles,
all that suffering and pain,
ordeals I hope no friend of mine
will ever have to undergo.

43

Sophocles

εἰ δὲ πικρούς, ἄναξ, ἔχθεις Ἀτρείδας,   510
ἐγὼ μέν, τὸ κείνων κακὸν τῷδε κέρδος
μετατιθέμενος, ἔνθαπερ ἐπιμέμονεν,   515
ἐπ᾽ εὐστόλου ταχείας νεὼς
πορεύσαιμ᾽ ἂν ἐς δόμους, τὰν θεῶν
νέμεσιν ἐκφυγών.

ΝΕΟΠΤΟΛΕΜΟΣ

ὅρα σὺ μὴ νῦν μέν τις εὐχερὴς παρῇς,
ὅταν δὲ πλησθῇς τῆς νόσου ξυνουσίᾳ,   520
τότ᾽ οὐκέθ᾽ αὑτὸς τοῖς λόγοις τούτοις φανῇς.

ΧΟΡΟΣ

ἥκιστα· τοῦτ᾽ οὐκ ἔσθ᾽ ὅπως ποτ᾽ εἰς ἐμὲ
τοὔνειδος ἕξεις ἐνδίκως ὀνειδίσαι.

ΝΕΟΠΤΟΛΕΜΟΣ

ἀλλ᾽ αἰσχρὰ μέντοι σοῦ γέ μ᾽ ἐνδεέστερον
ξένῳ φανῆναι πρὸς τὸ καίριον πονεῖν.   525
ἀλλ᾽ εἰ δοκεῖ, πλέωμεν, ὁρμάσθω ταχύς·
χἠ ναῦς γὰρ ἄξει κοὐκ ἀπαρνηθήσεται.
μόνον θεοὶ σῴζοιεν ἔκ τε τῆσδε γῆς
ἡμᾶς ὅποι τ᾽ ἐνθένδε βουλοίμεσθα πλεῖν.

ΦΙΛΟΚΤΗΤΗΣ

ὦ φίλτατον μὲν ἦμαρ, ἥδιστος δ᾽ ἀνήρ,   530
φίλοι δὲ ναῦται, πῶς ἂν ὑμὶν ἐμφανὴς
ἔργῳ γενοίμην, ὥς μ᾽ ἔθεσθε προσφιλῆ;
ἴωμεν, ὦ παῖ, προσκύσαντε τὴν ἔσω
ἄοικον εἰσοίκησιν, ὥς με καὶ μάθῃς
ἀφ᾽ ὧν διέζων ὥς τ᾽ ἔφυν εὐκάρδιος.   535
οἶμαι γὰρ οὐδ᾽ ἂν ὄμμασιν μόνην θέαν
ἄλλον λαβόντα πλὴν ἐμοῦ τλῆναι τάδε·
ἐγὼ δ᾽ ἀνάγκῃ προύμαθον στέργειν κακά.

44

And if, my lord, you hate [510]
those savage sons of Atreus,
I'd transform their evil acts
into some benefit for him
and carry him, as he has asked,
in your rapid well-stocked ship
back to his home, and so avoid
the righteous anger of the gods.

NEOPTOLEMUS
Take care—right now you're just a bystander.
That's easy. But later, when you've had your fill [520]
of that disease of his by living with it,
you may no longer stand by what you've said.

CHORUS
That will not happen. You'll never have just cause
to make that charge against me.

NEOPTOLEMUS
                              Well, I'd be shamed
if this stranger found me less prepared than you
to work on his behalf. So come on, then,
if it seems right to you, let's put to sea.
The man should start his trip without delay.
Our ship will take him. We will not refuse.
May the gods grant we safely leave this land
and sail from here wherever we may choose.

PHILOCTETES
What a glorious day! O you sweet man, [530]
and you dear sailors, I wish there was a way
to show you how you've made me your true friend!
Let's be gone, my lad, once we've kissed the ground
in ritual farewell to my home in there,
that was no home, so you can also learn
how I sustained myself, how I was born
with a determined heart. For I believe
the very sight of it would have convinced
anyone but me to give up this ordeal.
But from necessity I've had to learn
to bear such misery.

[Philoctetes starts to lead Neoptolemus up to his cave]

45

Sophocles

ΧΟΡΟΣ

ἐπίσχετον, μάθωμεν· ἄνδρε γὰρ δύο,
ὁ μὲν νεὼς σῆς ναυβάτης, ὁ δ' ἀλλόθρους,   540
χωρεῖτον, ὧν μαθόντες αὖθις εἴσιτον.

ΕΜΠΟΡΟΣ

Ἀχιλλέως παῖ, τόνδε τὸν ξυνέμπορον,
ὃς ἦν νεὼς σῆς σὺν δυοῖν ἄλλοιν φύλαξ,
ἐκέλευσ' ἐμοί σε ποῦ κυρῶν εἴης φράσαι,
ἐπείπερ ἀντέκυρσα, δοξάζων μὲν οὔ,   545
τύχῃ δέ πως πρὸς ταὐτὸν ὁρμισθεὶς πέδον.
πλέων γὰρ ὡς ναύκληρος οὐ πολλῷ στόλῳ
ἀπ' Ἰλίου πρὸς οἶκον ἐς τὴν εὔβοτρυν
Πεπάρηθον, ὡς ἤκουσα τοὺς ναύτας ὅτι
σοὶ πάντες εἶεν συννεναυστοληκότες,   550
ἔδοξέ μοι μὴ σῖγα, πρὶν φράσαιμί σοι,
τὸν πλοῦν ποεῖσθαι, προστυχόντι τῶν ἴσων.
οὐδὲν σύ που κάτοισθα τῶν σαυτοῦ πέρι,
ἃ τοῖσιν Ἀργείοισιν ἀμφὶ σοῦ νέα
βουλεύματ' ἐστί, κοὐ μόνον βουλεύματα,   555
ἀλλ' ἔργα δρώμεν', οὐκέτ' ἐξαργούμενα.

ΝΕΟΠΤΟΛΕΜΟΣ

ἀλλ' ἡ χάρις μὲν τῆς προμηθίας, ξένε,
εἰ μὴ κακὸς πέφυκα, προσφιλὴς μενεῖ·
φράσον δ' ἅπερ, γ' ἔλεξας, ὡς μάθω τί μοι
νεώτερον, βούλευμ' ἀπ' Ἀργείων ἔχεις.   560

ΕΜΠΟΡΟΣ

φροῦδοι διώκοντές σε ναυτικῷ στόλῳ
φοῖνιξ ὁ πρέσβυς οἵ τε Θησέως κόροι.

ΝΕΟΠΤΟΛΕΜΟΣ

ὡς ἐκ βίας μ' ἄξοντες ἢ λόγοις πάλιν;

46

CHORUS

Wait a moment!
Two men are coming. We should talk to them.
One's a sailor from your ship, the other one   [540]
a stranger. Let's hear what they may have to say.
Then you can go inside.

[A sailor enters, leading a spy disguised as a Merchant]

Merchant

Son of Achilles,
I asked my companion here, who was on watch,
guarding your ship with two other sailors,
to tell me where I might run into you.
I did not intend to have this meeting,
since I was driven to this very coast
by chance. I've been sailing my own ship
without much company on my way home,
back from Troy to wine-rich Peparethus.
But once I heard that all these sailors here   [550]
were from your crew, it seemed a good idea
to say something, not to resume my trip,
until I'd talked to you and then received
a fair reward. You may not understand
some matters which concern you—the Argives
have new things in store for you, not just plans
but actions they've already set in motion,
no longer mere ideas.

NEOPTOLEMUS

If I'm a worthy man,
stranger, this favour you are doing for me
by your concern will make me your good friend.
So tell me of these things you spoke about.
I need to understand just what you know
about the latest schemes the Argives have.   [560]

MERCHANT

Old Phoenix and the sons of Theseus
have set sail with a naval escort—
they're coming after you.

NEOPTOLEMUS

To take me back by force,
or to persuade me to return with them?

Sophocles

ΕΜΠΟΡΟΣ

οὐκ οἶδ'· ἀκούσας δ' ἄγγελος πάρειμί σοι.

ΝΕΟΠΤΟΛΕΜΟΣ

ἦ ταῦτα δὴ Φοῖνίξ τε χοὶ ξυνναυβάται   565
οὕτω καθ' ὁρμὴν δρῶσιν Ἀτρειδῶν χάριν;

ΕΜΠΟΡΟΣ

ὡς ταῦτ' ἐπίστω δρώμεν', οὐ μέλλοντ' ἔτι.

ΝΕΟΠΤΟΛΕΜΟΣ

πῶς οὖν Ὀδυσσεὺς πρὸς τάδ' οὐκ αὐτάγγελος
πλεῖν ἦν ἕτοιμος; ἦ φόβος τις εἶργέ νιν;

ΕΜΠΟΡΟΣ

κεῖνός γ' ἐπ' ἄλλον ἄνδρ' ὁ Τυδέως τε παῖς   570
ἔστελλον, ἡνίκ' ἐξανηγόμην ἐγώ.

ΝΕΟΠΤΟΛΕΜΟΣ

πρὸς ποῖον αὖ τόνδ' αὐτὸς Οὐδυσσεὺς ἔπλει;

ΕΜΠΟΡΟΣ

ἦν δή τις—ἀλλὰ τόνδε μοι πρῶτον φράσον
τίς ἐστίν· ἂν λέγῃς δὲ μὴ φώνει μέγα.

ΝΕΟΠΤΟΛΕΜΟΣ

ὅδ' ἔσθ' ὁ κλεινός σοι Φιλοκτήτης, ξένε.   575

ΕΜΠΟΡΟΣ

μή νύν μ' ἔρῃ τὰ πλείον', ἀλλ' ὅσον τάχος
ἔκπλει σεαυτὸν ξυλλαβὼν ἐκ τῆσδε γῆς.

ΦΙΛΟΚΤΗΤΗΣ

τί φησιν, ὦ παῖ; τί με κατὰ σκότον ποτὲ
διεμπολᾷ λόγοισι πρός σ' ὁ ναυβάτης;

MERCHANT

    I don't know. I'm here to tell you what I heard.

NEOPTOLEMUS

    Are Phoenix and his comrades on the ship
    so keen to do a favour for those men,
    the sons of Atreus?

MERCHANT

                    You can be sure
    they're doing it, not wasting any time.

NEOPTOLEMUS

    How come Odysseus was not prepared
    to make this trip and bring the news himself?
    Did some fear hold him back?

MERCHANT

               He was getting ready,   [570]
    along with Tydeus' son, to apprehend
    some other man, just as I was leaving.[13]

NEOPTOLEMUS

    What kind of person was Odysseus chasing?

MERCHANT

    He was a man. . .

[The Merchant pauses and nods towards Philoctetes]

              . . . but first of all tell me
    who this man is. And keep your voice down
    when you speak.

NEOPTOLEMUS

            This man here in front of you,
    stranger, is the famous Philoctetes.

MERCHANT

    Then question me no more. Get out of here.
    Sail from this place as quickly as you can.

PHILOCTETES

    What's he saying, my boy? Why is this sailor
    trying to haggle with you about me
    in the shadows?

ΝΕΟΠΤΟΛΕΜΟΣ

οὐκ οἶδά πω τί φησι· δεῖ δ᾽ αὐτὸν λέγειν　　　　580
εἰς φῶς ὃ λέξει, πρὸς σὲ κἀμὲ τούσδε τε.

ΕΜΠΟΡΟΣ

ὦ σπέρμ᾽ Ἀχιλλέως, μή με διαβάλῃς στρατῷ
λέγονθ᾽ ἃ μὴ δεῖ· πόλλ᾽ ἐγὼ κείνων ὕπο
δρῶν ἀντιπάσχω χρηστά θ᾽, οἷ᾽ ἀνὴρ πένης.

ΝΕΟΠΤΟΛΕΜΟΣ

ἐγώ εἰμ᾽ Ἀτρείδαις δυσμενής· οὗτος δέ μοι　　　585
φίλος μέγιστος, οὕνεκ᾽ Ἀτρείδας στυγεῖ.
δεῖ δή σ᾽ ἔμοιγ᾽ ἐλθόντα προσφιλῆ, λόγων
κρύψαι πρὸς ἡμᾶς μηδέν᾽ ὧν ἀκήκοας.

ΕΜΠΟΡΟΣ

ὅρα τί ποιεῖς, παῖ.

ΝΕΟΠΤΟΛΕΜΟΣ

　　　　　　　σκοπῶ κἀγὼ πάλαι.

ΕΜΠΟΡΟΣ

σὲ θήσομαι τῶνδ᾽ αἴτιον.　　　　　　　590

ΝΕΟΠΤΟΛΕΜΟΣ

　　　　　　　ποιοῦ λέγων.

ΕΜΠΟΡΟΣ

λέγω. ᾽πὶ τοῦτον ἄνδρε τώδ᾽ ὥπερ κλύεις,
ὁ Τυδέως παῖς ἥ τ᾽ Ὀδυσσέως βία,
διώμοτοι πλέουσιν ἦ μὴν ἢ λόγῳ
πείσαντες ἄξειν ἢ πρὸς ἰσχύος κράτος.
καὶ ταῦτ᾽ Ἀχαιοὶ πάντες ἤκουον σαφῶς　　　595
Ὀδυσσέως λέγοντος· οὗτος γὰρ πλέον
τὸ θάρσος εἶχε θατέρου δράσειν τάδε.

NEOPTOLEMUS
                I don't know what he means.   [580]
    But what he says, he must speak openly,
    to me, to you, and to the crew, as well.

MERCHANT
    Seed of Achilles, don't make the army
    angry at me for saying what I should not,
    since I get many benefits from them
    as payback for the services I give,
    the sorts of things a poor man carries out.

NEOPTOLEMUS
    Those sons of Atreus are my enemies.
    This man hates them, too—that's the reason
    he's my greatest friend. You've come here
    out of a sense of comradeship with me,
    so when you speak, you must not hide from us
    anything you heard.

MERCHANT
                Think of what you're doing.

NEOPTOLEMUS
    I have been thinking of that for some time.

MERCHANT
    I'll hold you responsible. . . .   [590]

NEOPTOLEMUS
                All right. Speak up.

MERCHANT
    Then I'll explain it to you. That man there—
    he's the one the two of them are chasing,
    those men I spoke of, cruel Odysseus
    and Diomedes, son of Tydeus.
    They've sworn an oath to sail and bring him back,
    either by persuading him with reasons
    or by overpowering force. All Achaeans
    clearly heard Odysseus when he said that.
    He was confident they'd be successful,
    much more than his comrade Diomedes.

Sophocles

ΝΕΟΠΤΟΛΕΜΟΣ

τίνος δ' Ἀτρεῖδαι τοῦδ' ἄγαν οὕτω χρόνῳ
τοσῷδ' ἐπεστρέφοντο πράγματος χάριν,
ὅν γ' εἶχον ἤδη χρόνιον ἐκβεβληκότες;   600
τίς ὁ πόθος αὐτοὺς ἵκετ'; ἢ θεῶν βία
καὶ νέμεσις, οἵπερ ἔργ' ἀμύνουσιν κακά;

ΕΜΠΟΡΟΣ

ἐγώ σε τοῦτ', ἴσως γὰρ οὐκ ἀκήκοας,
πᾶν ἐκδιδάξω. μάντις ἦν τις εὐγενής,
Πριάμου μὲν υἱός, ὄνομα δ' ὠνομάζετο   605
Ἕλενος, ὃν οὗτος νυκτὸς ἐξελθὼν μόνος,
ὁ πάντ' ἀκούων αἰσχρὰ καὶ λωβήτ' ἔπη
δόλιος Ὀδυσσεὺς εἷλε· δέσμιόν τ' ἄγων
ἔδειξ' Ἀχαιοῖς ἐς μέσον, θήραν καλήν·
ὃς δὴ τά τ' ἄλλ' αὐτοῖσι πάντ' ἐθέσπισεν   610
καὶ τἀπὶ Τροίᾳ πέργαμ' ὡς οὐ μή ποτε
πέρσοιεν, εἰ μὴ τόνδε πείσαντες λόγῳ
ἄγοιντο νήσου τῆσδ' ἐφ' ἧς ναίει τανῦν.
καὶ ταῦθ' ὅπως ἤκουσ' ὁ Λαέρτου τόκος
τὸν μάντιν εἰπόντ', εὐθέως ὑπέσχετο   615
τὸν ἄνδρ' Ἀχαιοῖς τόνδε δηλώσειν ἄγων·
οἴοιτο μὲν μάλισθ' ἑκούσιον λαβών,
εἰ μὴ θέλοι δ', ἄκοντα· καὶ τούτων κάρα
τέμνειν ἐφεῖτο τῷ θέλοντι μὴ τυχών.
ἤκουσας, ὦ παῖ, πάντα· τὸ σπεύδειν δέ σοι   620
καὐτῷ παραινῶ κεἴ τινος κήδει πέρι.

ΦΙΛΟΚΤΗΤΗΣ

οἴμοι τάλας· ἦ κεῖνος, ἡ πᾶσα βλάβη,
ἔμ' εἰς Ἀχαιοὺς ὤμοσεν πείσας στελεῖν;

52

NEOPTOLEMUS

    Why were the sons of Atreus so keen
    after all this time to redirect their thoughts
    onto this man, whom they'd kept in exile   [600]
    for so many years. What's got hold of them?
    What do they want? Or is it some power
    from the gods, a force of retribution,
    making them pay for evils they have done?

MERCHANT

    That's something you have probably not heard,
    so I'll explain it all. There was a prophet—
    his name was Helenus—of noble birth,
    a son of Priam. One night Odysseus,
    who has a reputation for deceit
    and every kind of shame, went out alone
    and used his trickery to capture him.
    Odysseus tied him up and brought him back,
    then put him on display among the Argives,
    like a splendid captured beast. Well, Helenus
    foretold all sorts of thing to them and then,   [610]
    he made this prophecy concerning Troy—
    they'd never smash its mighty citadel
    unless they could persuade Philoctetes,
    reason with him, and lead him back to Troy
    from the island which he now inhabits.
    Once he'd heard this prophecy from Helenus,
    Odysseus quickly promised he'd get him
    and show him to the Argives. He believed
    he'd bring Philoctetes with his consent—
    that was the likeliest scenario—
    but if he was unwilling, he'd use force.
    And then he said if he did not succeed,
    anyone who wished should cut his head off.
    Now, boy, you've heard it all, and I'd advise   [620]
    that you and anyone you care about
    act now without delay.

PHILOCTETES

                      That's bad news for me.
    Has that man, that source of every injury,
    sworn that he'll convince me to return,
    go back to the Achaeans? If I do,

Sophocles

πεισθήσομαι γὰρ ὧδε κἀξ Ἅιδου θανὼν
πρὸς φῶς ἀνελθεῖν, ὥσπερ οὐκείνου πατήρ.   625

ΕΜΠΟΡΟΣ
οὐκ οἶδ᾽ ἐγὼ ταῦτ᾽· ἀλλ᾽ ἐγὼ μὲν εἴμ᾽ ἐπὶ
ναῦν, σφῷν δ᾽ ὅπως ἄριστα συμφέροι θεός.

ΦΙΛΟΚΤΗΤΗΣ
οὔκουν τάδ᾽, ὦ παῖ, δεινά, τὸν Λαερτίου
ἔμ᾽ ἐλπίσαι ποτ᾽ ἂν λόγοισι μαλθακοῖς
δεῖξαι νεὼς ἄγοντ᾽ ἐν Ἀργείοις μέσοις;   630
οὔ· θᾶσσον ἂν τῆς πλεῖστον ἐχθίστης ἐμοὶ
κλύοιμ᾽ ἐχίδνης, ἥ μ᾽ ἔθηκεν ὧδ᾽ ἄπουν.
ἀλλ᾽ ἔστ᾽ ἐκείνῳ πάντα λεκτά, πάντα δὲ
τολμητά· καὶ νῦν οἶδ᾽ ὁθούνεχ᾽ ἵξεται.
ἀλλ᾽, ὦ τέκνον, χωρῶμεν, ὡς ἡμᾶς πολὺ   635
πέλαγος ὁρίζῃ τῆς Ὀδυσσέως νεώς.
ἴωμεν· ἥ τοι καίριος σπουδὴ πόνου
λήξαντος ὕπνον κἀνάπαυλαν ἤγαγεν.

ΝΕΟΠΤΟΛΕΜΟΣ
οὐκοῦν ἐπειδὰν πνεῦμα τοὐκ πρῴρας ἀνῇ,
τότε στελοῦμεν· νῦν γὰρ ἀντιοστατεῖ.   640

ΦΙΛΟΚΤΗΤΗΣ
ἀεὶ καλὸς πλοῦς ἔσθ᾽, ὅταν φεύγῃς κακά.

ΝΕΟΠΤΟΛΕΜΟΣ
οὔκ, ἀλλὰ κἀκείνοισι ταῦτ᾽ ἐναντία.

ΦΙΛΟΚΤΗΤΗΣ
οὐκ ἔστι λῃσταῖς πνεῦμ᾽ ἐναντιούμενον,
ὅταν παρῇ κλέψαι τι χἁρπάσαι βίᾳ.

ΝΕΟΠΤΟΛΕΜΟΣ
ἀλλ᾽ εἰ δοκεῖ, χωρῶμεν, ἔνδοθεν λαβὼν   645
ὅτου σε χρεία καὶ πόθος μάλιστ᾽ ἔχει.

54

once I'm dead I'll be persuaded to rise up
into the light from Hades, just the way
his father did.[14]

MERCHANT
                    I don't know about all that.
But I'm going back to my own ship. I pray
that somehow god brings you the best of help.

[Exit Merchant]

PHILOCTETES
My boy, don't you think it is extremely odd
Odysseus would ever entertain the hope
his reassuring words could bring me back,
lead me from his ship, and then show me off
there in the middle of the Argives. No!   [630]
I'd rather listen to my greatest foe,
the worst of all, the snake that crippled me
and made me what I am. That Odysseus
will say anything and attempt them all.
So now I know he's sailing to this place.
Come, my lad we should get going from here,
so there's a wider stretch of sea between us
and Odysseus' ship. Let's go. Well-timed haste
brings sleep and rest after the work is done.

NEOPTOLEMUS
We'll set sail when the wind stops blowing in
right at our bow. Its course is now against us.   [640]

PHILOCTETES
But the moment one is fleeing trouble
is always the best time to put to sea.

NEOPTOLEMUS
No. This wind is blowing in their faces, too.

PHILOCTETES
There's no wind can hold back any pirates
when they're intent of plundering and theft
and using force.

NEOPTOLEMUS
                    Well, if that's what you think,
then let's be off, once you've taken from in there
the things you need or really want to keep.

Sophocles

ΦΙΛΟΚΤΗΤΗΣ
ἀλλ᾽ ἔστιν ὧν δεῖ, καίπερ οὐ πολλῶν ἄπο.

ΝΕΟΠΤΟΛΕΜΟΣ
τί τοῦθ᾽ ὃ μὴ νεώς γε τῆς ἐμῆς ἔπι;

ΦΙΛΟΚΤΗΤΗΣ
φύλλον τί μοι πάρεστιν, ᾧ μάλιστ᾽ ἀεὶ
κοιμῶ τόδ᾽ ἕλκος, ὥστε πραΰνειν πάνυ.   650

ΝΕΟΠΤΟΛΕΜΟΣ
ἀλλ᾽ ἔκφερ᾽ αὐτό. τί γὰρ ἔτ᾽ ἄλλ᾽ ἐρᾷς λαβεῖν;

ΦΙΛΟΚΤΗΤΗΣ
εἴ μοί τι τόξων τῶνδ᾽ ἀπημελημένον
παρερρύηκεν, ὡς λίπω μή τῳ λαβεῖν.

ΝΕΟΠΤΟΛΕΜΟΣ
ἦ ταῦτα γὰρ τὰ κλεινὰ τόξ᾽ ἃ νῦν ἔχεις;

ΦΙΛΟΚΤΗΤΗΣ
ταῦτ᾽, οὐ γὰρ ἄλλ᾽ ἔστ᾽, ἀλλ᾽ ἃ βαστάζω χεροῖν.   655

ΝΕΟΠΤΟΛΕΜΟΣ
ἆρ᾽ ἔστιν ὥστε κἀγγύθεν θέαν λαβεῖν
καὶ βαστάσαι με προσκύσαι θ᾽ ὥσπερ θεόν;

ΦΙΛΟΚΤΗΤΗΣ
σοί γ᾽, ὦ τέκνον, καὶ τοῦτο κἄλλο τῶν ἐμῶν
ὁποῖον ἄν σοι ξυμφέρῃ γενήσεται.

ΝΕΟΠΤΟΛΕΜΟΣ
καὶ μὴν ἐρῶ γε, τὸν δ᾽ ἔρωθ᾽ οὕτως ἔχω·   660
εἴ μοι θέμις, θέλοιμ᾽ ἄν· εἰ δὲ μή, πάρες.

ΦΙΛΟΚΤΗΤΗΣ
ὅσιά τε φωνεῖς ἔστι τ᾽, ὦ τέκνον, θέμις,
ὅς γ᾽ ἡλίου τόδ᾽ εἰσορᾶν ἐμοὶ φάος

PHILOCTETES
    Some things are necessary, but not much.

NEOPTOLEMUS
    What's there that we won't have on board my ship?

PHILOCTETES
    I have a certain herb I always use,
    the most effective treatment for this wound   [650]
    until it is completely cured.

NEOPTOLEMUS
                                Bring that.
    Is there something else you want to get?

PHILOCTETES
    Any of the arrows I've forgotten
    or overlooked, in case I leave them there
    for someone else to take.

NEOPTOLEMUS
                        What you're holding there—
    is that the famous bow?

PHILOCTETES
                                The very one.
    This weapon in my hands is not a substitute.

NEOPTOLEMUS
    Is there some way I could inspect the bow
    more closely, hold it, get a feel for it
    as something sacred?

PHILOCTETES
                        For you alone, my son,
    I'll grant this wish and whatever else I can
    that's in your interest.

NEOPTOLEMUS
                        I'd love to hold it,   [660]
    but I want that only if it's lawful.
    If not, you should forget I ever asked.

PHILOCTETES
    What you say, my boy, is just and pious.
    You're the only one who's offered me
    the light of life, the hope that I will see

μόνος δέδωκας, ὃς χθόν' Οἰταίαν ἰδεῖν,
ὃς πατέρα πρέσβυν, ὃς φίλους, ὃς τῶν ἐμῶν   665
ἐχθρῶν μ' ἔνερθεν ὄντ' ἀνέστησας πέρα.
θάρσει, παρέσται ταῦτά σοι καὶ θιγγάνειν
καὶ δόντι δοῦναι κἀξεπεύξασθαι βροτῶν
ἀρετῆς ἕκατι τῶνδ' ἐπιψαῦσαι μόνον·
εὐεργετῶν γὰρ καὐτὸς αὔτ' ἐκτησάμην.   670

ΝΕΟΠΤΟΛΕΜΟΣ
οὐκ ἄχθομαί σ' ἰδών τε καὶ λαβὼν φίλον·
ὅστις γὰρ εὖ δρᾶν εὖ παθὼν ἐπίσταται,
παντὸς γένοιτ' ἂν κτήματος κρείσσων φίλος.
χωροῖς ἂν εἴσω.

ΦΙΛΟΚΤΗΤΗΣ
                    καὶ σέ γ' εἰσάξω· τὸ γὰρ
νοσοῦν ποθεῖ σε ξυμπαραστάτην λαβεῖν.   675

ΧΟΡΟΣ
λόγῳ μὲν ἐξήκουσ', ὄπωπα δ' οὐ μάλα,
τὸν πελάταν λέκτρων ποτὲ τῶν Διὸς
κατὰ δρομάδ' ἄμπυκα δέσμιον ὡς ἔβαλεν παγκρατὴς
    Κρόνου παῖς·   680
ἄλλον δ' οὔτιν' ἔγωγ' οἶδα κλύων οὐδ' ἐσιδὼν μοίρᾳ
τοῦδ' ἐχθίονι συντυχόντα
θνατῶν, ὃς οὔτ' ἔρξας τιν' οὔ τι νοσφίσας,
ἀλλ' ἴσος ὢν ἴσοις ἀνήρ,   685
ὤλλυθ' ὧδ' ἀναξίως.
τόδε τοι θαῦμά μ' ἔχει,
πῶς ποτε πῶς ποτ' ἀμφιπλάκτων ῥοθίων μόνος κλύων,
    πῶς ἄρα πανδάκρυτον οὕτω βιοτὰν κατέσχεν·   690

the land of Oeta, my aged father,
and my friends. When I was lying there,
at my enemies' feet, you raised me up
beyond their reach. Take courage. This bow
is yours to hold and then give back to me,
the one who gave it to you. You can claim,
thanks to your virtue, you're the only man
who's touched it. That's the reason I myself
acquired the bow—by acting virtuously.[15]   [670]

NEOPTOLEMUS
I'm glad I found you and became your friend.
A man who knows how to return a favour
for a favour he's received has proved himself
a friend more valuable than all possessions.
Please go inside.

PHILOCTETES
                    I'll go in there with you.
My sick condition craves your company.

[Philoctetes and Neoptolemus enter the cave together]

CHORUS
Though I never saw it happen,
I have heard the distant rumour
how a man once stole into
the marriage bed of Zeus—and then
how the mighty son of Cronos
lashed him to a whirling wheel.[16]
But from all I've heard and seen   [680]
I know no other mortal man
who's run into a fate as harsh
as has Philoctetes, a man
who did no wrong to anyone
by thievery or violence,
but acted fairly towards those
who treated him respectfully,
and then, without deserving it,
he was abandoned here to die.
Amazement seizes me to think
how, as he listened by himself
to breakers crashing on the shore,
he somehow kept a hold on life,   [690]
which brought him so much pain.

59

ἵν' αὐτὸς ἦν πρόσουρος, οὐκ ἔχων βάσιν,

οὐδέ τιν' ἐγχώρων κακογείτονα,

παρ' ᾧ στόνον ἀντίτυπον βαρυβρῶτ' ἀποκλαύσειεν

    αἱματηρόν·

ὃς τὰν θερμοτάταν αἱμάδα κηκιομέναν ἑλκέων   696

ἐνθήρου ποδὸς ἠπίοισι

φύλλοις κατευνάσειεν, εἴ τις ἐμπέσοι,

φορβάδος ἐκ γαίας ἑλών·   700

εἶρπε γὰρ ἄλλοτ' ἀλλαχᾷ

τότ' ἂν εἰλυόμενος

παῖς ἄτερ ὡς φίλας τιθήνας ὅθεν εὐμάρει' ὑπάρχοι

    πόρου, ἀνίκ' ἐξανείη δακέθυμος ἄτα·   705

οὐ φορβὰν ἱερᾶς γᾶς σπόρον, οὐκ ἄλλων

αἴρων τῶν νεμόμεσθ' ἀνέρες ἀλφησταί,

πλὴν ἐξ ὠκυβόλων εἴ ποτε τόξων   710

πτανοῖς ἰοῖς ἀνύσειε γαστρὶ φορβάν.

    ὦ μελέα ψυχά,

ὃς μηδ' οἰνοχύτου πώματος ἥσθη δεκέτει χρόνῳ,

λεύσσων δ' ὅπου γνοίη στατὸν εἰς ὕδωρ,   716

    ἀεὶ προσενώμα.

νῦν δ' ἀνδρῶν ἀγαθῶν παιδὸς ὑπαντήσας

εὐδαίμων ἀνύσει καὶ μέγας ἐκ κείνων·   720

ὅς νιν ποντοπόρῳ δούρατι, πλήθει

πολλῶν μηνῶν, πατρίαν ἄγει πρὸς αὐλὰν

    Μαλιάδων νυμφᾶν   725

He had no neighbour but himself
and lacked the power to walk. No one
for a companion in the place
throughout his illness, no one there
to answer him with sympathy
when he cried out against the plague
that ate his flesh and made him bleed,
no one to gather healing leaves
when he succumbed to an attack,
to take them from the fertile earth   [700]
and staunch the burning streams of blood
oozing from the ulcerous sores
on his wounded foot. No. He crept
back and forth, crawling like a child
with no dear nurse attending him,
to any place where he might find
relief to ease his pain, and then
his all-consuming agonies
eventually would subside.

And he could not collect his food
by taking what the earth provides
or any other nourishment
for those of us who feed ourselves
with our own work, except those times   [710]
he eased his hunger with a meal
he got himself with feathered arrows
from his swiftly striking bow.
He's lived a miserable life,
without the joy of succouring wine,
but always for the past ten years
he's had to look around and find
whatever puddles he could reach.

But now, with all these troubles past,
he'll find success and happiness.   [720]
He's met a noble family's son
who'll take him, after all this time,
aboard his own seaworthy boat
and sail to his ancestral home,
the place where nymphs of Malis dwell,

Σπερχειοῦ τε παρ' ὄχθας, ἵν' ὁ χάλκασπις ἀνὴρ θεοῖς
πλάθει πατρὸς θείῳ πυρὶ παμφαής,
  Οἴτας ὑπὲρ ὄχθων.

ΝΕΟΠΤΟΛΕΜΟΣ
  ἕρπ', εἰ θέλεις. τί δή ποθ' ὧδ' ἐξ οὐδενὸς   730
  λόγου σιωπᾷς κἀπόπληκτος ὧδ' ἔχει;

ΦΙΛΟΚΤΗΤΗΣ
  ἀᾶ, ἀᾶ.

ΝΕΟΠΤΟΛΕΜΟΣ
  τί δ' ἔστιν;

ΦΙΛΟΚΤΗΤΗΣ
      οὐδὲν δεινόν· ἀλλ' ἴθ', ὦ τέκνον.

ΝΕΟΠΤΟΛΕΜΟΣ
  μῶν ἄλγος ἴσχεις τῆς παρεστώσης νόσου;

ΦΙΛΟΚΤΗΤΗΣ
  οὐ δῆτ' ἔγωγ', ἀλλ' ἄρτι κουφίζειν δοκῶ.   735
  ὦ θεοί.

ΝΕΟΠΤΟΛΕΜΟΣ
  τί τοὺς θεοὺς ὧδ' ἀναστένων καλεῖς;

ΦΙΛΟΚΤΗΤΗΣ
  σωτῆρας αὐτοὺς ἠπίους θ' ἡμῖν μολεῖν.
  ἀᾶ, ἀᾶ.

ΝΕΟΠΤΟΛΕΜΟΣ
  τί ποτε πέπονθας; οὐκ ἐρεῖς, ἀλλ' ὧδ' ἔσει   740
  σιγηλός; ἐν κακῷ δέ τῳ φαίνει κυρῶν.

ΦΙΛΟΚΤΗΤΗΣ
  ἀπόλωλα, τέκνον, κοὐ δυνήσομαι κακὸν
  κρύψαι παρ' ὑμῖν, ἀτταταῖ· διέρχεται

along Spercheius river banks,
where, high up on Oeta's heights,
that bronze-shield warrior rose up,
and moved up to the gods, ablaze
in his own father's sacred fire.[17]

[NEOPTOLEMUS and PHILOCTETES come out from the cave.
PHILOCTETES is carrying his bow and is in obvious pain]

NEOPTOLEMUS

Let's move out of here, if that's what you desire.   [730]
Why are you so silent? There's no need for that.
Have you been paralyzed?

PHILOCTETES

        Aaiiii . . . aaiii.

NEOPTOLEMUS

What's wrong?

PHILOCTETES

             It's nothing serious, my boy.
Just keep going.

NEOPTOLEMUS

                   Are you in agony
from that disease which always bothers you?

PHILOCTETES

No, no. I think it's better now. O you gods!

NEOPTOLEMUS

Why scream like that and call out to the gods?

PHILOCTETES

For them to come to me in person . . . save me . . .
Aaaiiiiii! . . . Aaaaaaiiiiii!!! . . . Aaaaaiiiiiiiiii!

NEOPTOLEMUS

What's troubling you now? Why not speak up?   [740]
Why don't you tell me? It's obvious enough
you're in some kind of pain.

PHILOCTETES

               I'm done for, my boy.
I can't conceal this dreadful thing from you . . .
Aaiiii . . . It goes right through me . . . shooting pains.

διέρχεται. δύστηνος, ὦ τάλας ἐγώ.
ἀπόλωλα, τέκνον· βρύκομαι, τέκνον· παπαῖ,   745
ἀπαππαπαῖ, παπαππαπαππαπαππαπαῖ.
πρὸς θεῶν, πρόχειρον εἴ τί σοι, τέκνον, πάρα
ξίφος χεροῖν, πάταξον εἰς ἄκρον πόδα·
ἀπάμησον ὡς τάχιστα· μὴ φείσῃ βίου.
ἴθ᾽, ὦ παῖ.   750

ΝΕΟΠΤΟΛΕΜΟΣ
τί δ᾽ ἔστιν οὕτω νεοχμὸν ἐξαίφνης, ὅτου
τοσήνδ᾽ ἰυγὴν καὶ στόνον σαυτοῦ ποεῖ;

ΦΙΛΟΚΤΗΤΗΣ
οἶσθ᾽, ὦ τέκνον;

ΝΕΟΠΤΟΛΕΜΟΣ
τί δ᾽ ἔστιν;

ΦΙΛΟΚΤΗΤΗΣ
οἶσθ᾽, ὦ παῖ;

ΝΕΟΠΤΟΛΕΜΟΣ
τί σοί;
οὐκ οἶδα.

ΦΙΛΟΚΤΗΤΗΣ
πῶς οὐκ οἶσθα; παππαπαππαπαῖ.

ΝΕΟΠΤΟΛΕΜΟΣ
δεινόν γε τοὐπίσαγμα τοῦ νοσήματος.   755

ΦΙΛΟΚΤΗΤΗΣ
δεινὸν γὰρ οὐδὲ ῥητόν· ἀλλ᾽ οἴκτιρέ με.

ΝΕΟΠΤΟΛΕΜΟΣ
τί δῆτα δράσω;

ΦΙΛΟΚΤΗΤΗΣ
μή με ταρβήσας προδῷς·
ἥκει γὰρ αὕτη διὰ χρόνου πλάνοις ἴσως
ὡς ἐξεπλήσθη.

It's horrible . . . I'm in such agony!
I'm being destroyed, my lad, eaten up . . .
O my god . . . my god . . . such awful pain!
O my boy, if you have got a sword at hand
by the gods, I beg you, slice my foot off,
here, where my leg ends. Amputate it now!
Don't worry about my life. Do it, my boy!   [750]

NEOPTOLEMUS

    What new pain makes you scream so suddenly?
    Why groan and cry like this?

PHILOCTETES

                You know, my son.

NEOPTOLEMUS

    What is it?

PHILOCTETES

            My boy, you know the reason.

NEOPTOLEMUS

    No, I don't. What's wrong with you?

PHILOCTETES

    How could you not know? Aaaaiiiii!

NEOPTOLEMUS

    It's the agonizing weight of your disease.

PHILOCTETES

    That's right . . . the pain . . . it's indescribable.
    Have pity on me!

NEOPTOLEMUS

            What shall I do?

PHILOCTETES

    Don't grow afraid and just give up on me.
    The disease attacks me only now and then,
    perhaps when it has finished roaming elsewhere.

Sophocles

ΝΕΟΠΤΟΛΕΜΟΣ
 ἰὼ ἰὼ δύστηνε σύ,
δύστηνε δῆτα διὰ πόνων πάντων φανείς. 760
βούλει λάβωμαι δῆτα καὶ θίγω τί σου;

ΦΙΛΟΚΤΗΤΗΣ
 μὴ δῆτα τοῦτό γ'· ἀλλά μοι τὰ τόξ' ἑλὼν
τάδ', ὥσπερ ᾐτοῦ μ' ἀρτίως, ἕως ἀνῇ
τὸ πῆμα τοῦτο τῆς νόσου τὸ νῦν παρόν, 765
σῷζ' αὐτὰ καὶ φύλασσε. λαμβάνει γὰρ οὖν
ὕπνος μ', ὅταν περ τὸ κακὸν ἐξίῃ τόδε·
κοὐκ ἔστι λῆξαι πρότερον· ἀλλ' ἐὰν χρεὼν
ἕκηλον εὕδειν. ἢν δὲ τῷδε τῷ χρόνῳ
μόλωσ' ἐκεῖνοι, πρὸς θεῶν ἐφίεμαι 770
ἑκόντα μηδ' ἄκοντα μηδέ τῳ τέχνῃ
κείνοις μεθεῖναι ταῦτα, μὴ σαυτόν θ' ἅμα
κἄμ', ὄντα σαυτοῦ πρόστροπον, κτείνας γένῃ.

ΝΕΟΠΤΟΛΕΜΟΣ
 θάρσει προνοίας οὕνεκ'· οὐ δοθήσεται
πλὴν σοί τε κἀμοί· ξὺν τύχῃ δὲ πρόσφερε. 775

ΦΙΛΟΚΤΗΤΗΣ
 ἰδοὺ δέχου, παῖ· τὸν φθόνον δὲ πρόσκυσον
μή σοι γενέσθαι πολύπον' αὐτὰ μηδ' ὅπως
ἐμοί τε καὶ τῷ πρόσθ' ἐμοῦ κεκτημένῳ.

ΝΕΟΠΤΟΛΕΜΟΣ
 ὦ θεοί, γένοιτο ταῦτα νῷν· γένοιτο δὲ
πλοῦς οὔριός τε κεὐσταλὴς ὅποι ποτὲ 780
θεὸς δικαιοῖ χὠ στόλος πορσύνεται.

ΦΙΛΟΚΤΗΤΗΣ
 ἀλλ' οὖν δέδοικα μὴ ἀτέλεστ' εὔχῃ, τέκνον.
στάζει γὰρ αὖ μοι φοίνιον τόδ' ἐκ βυθοῦ
κηκῖον αἷμα, καί τι προσδοκῶ νέον.
παπαῖ, φεῦ. 785

NEOPTOLEMUS

 Alas, you've had such a tormented life,
 poor man, it seems you've really suffered   [760]
 every kind of trouble. What do you want?
 Can I help you up? Do you need my hand?

PHILOCTETES

 No. Don't do that. But take this bow for me—
 you just asked if I would let you hold it.
 Make sure you guard it well. Keep it safe,
 until this present fit from my disease
 gets less intense. Once the pain relents,
 I'll be overcome with sleep—it won't leave
 before that time, so let me rest in peace.
 If those two men get here while I'm asleep,
 don't give them the bow—no, by the gods,   [770]
 I tell you don't—not of your own free will,
 or without wanting to, or through a trick—
 you may get yourself destroyed and me,
 and I'm your suppliant.

NEOPTOLEMUS

         Don't worry.
 I'll be careful. No one's hands will touch the bow
 but yours and mine. Let me take it from you,
 and may it bring good luck!

PHILOCTETES

        Here, lad, take it.
 Give the gods' jealousy due reverence,
 in case this bow brings you much suffering,
 as it has me and the man who owned it
 before I did.[18]

NEOPTOLEMUS

     Gods grant us both success—
 a prosperous quick trip to any place   [780]
 we come to on our trip which god thinks right.

PHILOCTETES *[still in great pain]*

 My boy, I'm afraid your prayers are useless.
 Dark red blood is dripping down, oozing out
 from deep within my sore, and I expect
 there'll be new attack. Aiiiii . . . aaaiii . . .

παπαῖ μάλ᾽, ὦ πούς, οἷά μ᾽ ἐργάσει κακά.
προσέρπει,
προσέρχεται τόδ᾽ ἐγγύς. οἴμοι μοι τάλας.
ἔχετε τὸ πρᾶγμα· μὴ φύγητε μηδαμῇ.
ἀτταταῖ.   790
ὦ ξένε Κεφαλλήν, εἴθε σου διαμπερὲς
στέρνων ἔχοιτ᾽ ἄλγησις ἥδε. φεῦ, παπαῖ,
παπαῖ μάλ᾽ αὖθις. ὦ διπλοῖ στρατηλάται,
Ἀγάμεμνον, ὦ Μενέλαε, πῶς ἂν ἀντ᾽ ἐμοῦ
τὸν ἴσον χρόνον τρέφοιτε τήνδε τὴν νόσον;   795
ἰώ μοι.
ὦ Θάνατε Θάνατε, πῶς ἀεὶ καλούμενος
οὕτω κατ᾽ ἦμαρ, οὐ δύνᾳ μολεῖν ποτε;
ὦ τέκνον ὦ γενναῖον, ἀλλὰ συλλαβὼν
τῷ Λημνίῳ τῷδ᾽ ἀνακαλουμένῳ πυρὶ   800
ἔμπρησον, ὦ γενναῖε· κἀγώ τοί ποτε
τὸν τοῦ Διὸς παῖδ᾽ ἀντὶ τῶνδε τῶν ὅπλων,
ἃ νῦν σὺ σῴζεις, τοῦτ᾽ ἐπηξίωσα δρᾶν.
τί φής, παῖ;
τί φής; τί σιγᾷς; ποῦ ποτ᾽ ὤν, τέκνον, κυρεῖς;   805

ΝΕΟΠΤΟΛΕΜΟΣ
    ἀλγῶ πάλαι δὴ τἀπὶ σοὶ στένων κακά.

ΦΙΛΟΚΤΗΤΗΣ
    ἀλλ᾽, ὦ τέκνον, καὶ θάρσος ἴσχ᾽· ὡς ἥδε μοι
    ὀξεῖα φοιτᾷ καὶ ταχεῖ᾽ ἀπέρχεται.
    ἀλλ᾽ ἀντιάζω, μή με καταλίπῃς μόνον.

ΝΕΟΠΤΟΛΕΜΟΣ
    θάρσει, μενοῦμεν.   810

ΦΙΛΟΚΤΗΤΗΣ
                        ἦ μενεῖς;

ΝΕΟΠΤΟΛΕΜΟΣ
                                    σαφῶς φρόνει.

ΦΙΛΟΚΤΗΤΗΣ
    οὐ μήν σ᾽ ἔνορκόν γ᾽ ἀξιῶ θέσθαι, τέκνον.

it's really bad . . . this accursed foot . . .
it keeps tormenting me . . . creeping up my limb . . .
it's almost here . . . aaiii, it hurts so much . . .
You know what's going on—don't abandon me,   [790]
don't leave . . . aaaaiiiii . . . Ah, Odysseus,
you who were once my guest, how I now wish
you were in such agony, with pains like this
driving through your chest! It's hard for me . . .
Aaaaiii . . . it strikes again! You two commanders—
you, Agamemnon and Menelaus,
may this disease feed on the pair of you
instead of me and for as many years . . .
It's too much for me . . . O death, death,
here I keep calling for you all the time.
Why can't you ever come? O noble boy,
my child, my welcome friend, take me away,
and burn me in that famous Lemnian fire.[19]   [800]
I thought it right to do that service once
for Zeus' son—and in return I got
those weapons you are holding for me now.
What do you say, lad? What do you say?
Why so quiet? What's on your mind, my son?

NEOPTOLEMUS
I feel so sorry for you—what you're going through
has for a long time now disturbed me.

PHILOCTETES
Don't worry about that, my lad. Cheer up.
These fits are nasty but they pass off soon.
So I beg you not to leave me here alone.

NEOPTOLEMUS
Don't be afraid. We'll stay.   [810]

PHILOCTETES
                              You will not leave?

NEOPTOLEMUS
You can be sure of it.

PHILOCTETES
                              Well, my lad,
I don't think it's fair to make you swear to it.

Sophocles

ΝΕΟΠΤΟΛΕΜΟΣ
ὡς οὐ θέμις γ᾽ ἐμοῦστι σοῦ μολεῖν ἄτερ.

ΦΙΛΟΚΤΗΤΗΣ
ἔμβαλλε χειρὸς πίστιν.

ΝΕΟΠΤΟΛΕΜΟΣ
ἐμβάλλω μενεῖν.

ΦΙΛΟΚΤΗΤΗΣ
ἐκεῖσε νῦν μ᾽, ἐκεῖσε

ΝΕΟΠΤΟΛΕΜΟΣ
ποῖ λέγεις;

ΦΙΛΟΚΤΗΤΗΣ
ἄνω

ΝΕΟΠΤΟΛΕΜΟΣ
τί παραφρονεῖς αὖ; τί τὸν ἄνω λεύσσεις κύκλον;   815

ΦΙΛΟΚΤΗΤΗΣ
μέθες μέθες με.

ΝΕΟΠΤΟΛΕΜΟΣ
ποῖ μεθῶ;

ΦΙΛΟΚΤΗΤΗΣ
μέθες ποτέ.

ΝΕΟΠΤΟΛΕΜΟΣ
οὔ φημ᾽ ἐάσειν.

ΦΙΛΟΚΤΗΤΗΣ
ἀπό μ᾽ ὀλεῖς, ἢν προσθίγῃς.

ΝΕΟΠΤΟΛΕΜΟΣ
καὶ δὴ μεθίημ᾽, εἴ τι δὴ πλέον φρονεῖς.

NEOPTOLEMUS
There's no need. It would be against the law
for me to go without you.

PHILOCTETES
                    Give me your hand—
a pledge of trust.

NEOPTOLEMUS
        I will stay. Here's my pledge.

*[NEOPTOLEMUS and PHILOCTETES shake hands. Then a new fit
attacks PHILOCTETES, and he falls to his knees]*

PHILOCTETES
Take me back . . . in there.

NEOPTOLEMUS
            Where do you mean?

PHILOCTETES *[indicating the opening to the cave above them]*
Up there . . . in there!

NEOPTOLEMUS *[grabbing Philoctetes]*
                        Is this another fit?
Why roll your eyes up at the sky?

PHILOCTETES
                    Let go!
Get your hands away from me!

NEOPTOLEMUS
                If I do,
where will you go?

PHILOCTETES
            Take your hands off me!

NEOPTOLEMUS
I won't do that, I tell you.

PHILOCTETES
                    You'll kill me
if you keep grabbing me!

NEOPTOLEMUS
                All right, I'll let go,
if you really think that's better for you.

Sophocles

ΦΙΛΟΚΤΗΤΗΣ

ὦ γαῖα, δέξαι θανάσιμόν μ' ὅπως ἔχω
τὸ γὰρ κακὸν τόδ' οὐκέτ' ὀρθοῦσθαί μ' ἐᾷ.   820

ΝΕΟΠΤΟΛΕΜΟΣ

τὸν ἄνδρ' ἔοικεν ὕπνος οὐ μακροῦ χρόνου
ἕξειν· κάρα γὰρ ὑπτιάζεται τόδε·
ἱδρώς γέ τοί νιν πᾶν καταστάζει δέμας,
μέλαινά τ' ἄκρου τις παρέρρωγεν ποδὸς
αἱμορραγὴς φλέψ. ἀλλ' ἐάσωμεν, φίλοι,   825
ἔκηλον αὐτόν, ὡς ἂν εἰς ὕπνον πέσῃ.

ΧΟΡΟΣ

Ὕπν' ὀδύνας ἀδαής, Ὕπνε δ' ἀλγέων,
εὐαὲς ἡμῖν ἔλθοις,
εὐαίων εὐαίων, ὦναξ·
ὄμμασι δ' ἀντίσχοις   830
τάνδ' αἴγλαν, ἃ τέταται τανῦν.
ἴθι ἴθι μοι παιών.

ὦ τέκνον, ὅρα ποῦ στάσει,
ποῖ δέ μοι τἀνθένδε βάσει,
φροντίδος. ὁρᾷς ἤδη.   835
πρὸς τί μενοῦμεν πράσσειν;
καιρός τοι πάντων γνώμαν ἴσχων
πολύ τι πολὺ παρὰ πόδα κράτος ἄρνυται.

ΝΕΟΠΤΟΛΕΜΟΣ

ἀλλ' ὅδε μὲν κλύει οὐδέν, ἐγὼ δ' ὁρῶ οὕνεκα θήραν
τήνδ' ἁλίως ἔχομεν τόξων, δίχα τοῦδε πλέοντες.   840
τοῦδε γὰρ ὁ στέφανος, τοῦτον θεὸς εἶπε κομίζειν.
κομπεῖν δ' ἔστ' ἀτελῆ σὺν ψεύδεσιν αἰσχρὸν ὄνειδος.

ΧΟΡΟΣ

ἀλλά, τέκνον, τάδε μὲν θεὸς ὄψεται·
ὧν δ' ἂν ἀμείβῃ μ' αὖθις,
βαιάν μοι, βαιάν, ὦ τέκνον,   845
πέμπε λόγων φάμαν·

72

PHILOCTETES
    I'm close to death—O Earth, embrace me now!—
    these fits won't let me stand up any more.   [820]

[PHILOCTETES collapses prone on the ground]

NEOPTOLEMUS
    I think sleep will overcome him soon.
    His head is sinking back. His whole body
    is soaked in sweat, and a black flow of blood
    has burst through on his heel. Leave him alone,
    my friends, so he can fall asleep.

CHORUS
    O Sleep who knows no pain,
    sweet Sleep so free of suffering,
    come to us with joy, my king,
    and bring him happiness.
    Hold before his eyes that light   [830]
    which shines around them now.
    Come down, I pray, and heal him.

    My son, think about where you are right now
    and how you sort out where we go from here.
    Do you not see him there? He's asleep. Let's act.
    Why hesitate? For Opportunity,
    which takes everything into account,
    often wins decisively in one quick blow.

NEOPTOLEMUS *[looking down at sleeping Philoctetes]*
    He cannot hear a thing. But even so,
    I know if we set off without this man,   [840]
    we'll have hunted down this bow in vain.
    The crown of victory belongs to him—
    the god instructed us to lead him back.
    We'll bring disgrace and shame upon ourselves,
    boasting of what we did, when the result
    was incomplete and when we lied, as well.

CHORUS
    But the god will see to that, my boy.
    And when you answer me again
    you must whisper to me, lad,
    speak softly when you talk.

73

Sophocles

ὡς πάντων ἐν νόσῳ εὐδρακὴς
ὕπνος ἄϋπνος λεύσσειν.
ἀλλ᾿ ὅτι δύνᾳ μάκιστον
κεῖνο δή μοι κεῖνο λάθρᾳ   850
ἐξιδοῦ ὅπᾳ πράξεις.
οἶσθα γὰρ ἂν αὐδῶμαι,
εἰ ταύταν τούτων γνώμαν ἴσχεις,
μάλα τοι ἄπορα πυκινοῖς ἐνιδεῖν πάθη.
οὖρός τοι, τέκνον, οὖρος·   855
ἀνὴρ δ᾿ ἀνόμματος οὐδ᾿ ἔχων
ἀρωγὰν ἐκτέταται νύχιος,
(ἀλεὴς ὕπνος ἐσθλός,)
οὐ χερός, οὐ ποδός, οὔ τινος ἄρχων,   860
ἀλλά τις ὡς Ἀΐδᾳ παρακείμενος.
ὅρα, βλέπ᾿ εἰ καίρια
φθέγγει· τὸ δ᾿ ἁλώσιμον
ἐμᾷ φροντίδι, παῖ,   863β
πόνος ὁ μὴ φοβῶν κράτιστος.

ΝΕΟΠΤΟΛΕΜΟΣ
σιγᾶν κελεύω μηδ᾿ ἀφεστάναι φρενῶν·   865
κινεῖ γὰρ ἀνὴρ ὄμμα κἀνάγει κάρα.

ΦΙΛΟΚΤΗΤΗΣ
ὦ φέγγος ὕπνου διάδοχον τό τ᾿ ἐλπίδων
ἄπιστον οἰκούρημα τῶνδε τῶν ξένων.
οὐ γάρ ποτ᾿, ὦ παῖ, τοῦτ᾿ ἂν ἐξηύχησ᾿ ἐγώ,
τλῆναί σ᾿ ἐλεινῶς ὧδε τἀμὰ πήματα   870
μεῖναι παρόντα καὶ ξυνωφελοῦντά μοι.
οὔκουν Ἀτρεῖδαι τοῦτ᾿ ἔτλησαν εὐφόρως
οὕτως ἐνεγκεῖν, ἀγαθοὶ στρατηλάται.
ἀλλ᾿ εὐγενὴς γὰρ ἡ φύσις κἀξ εὐγενῶν,
ὦ τέκνον, ἡ σή, πάντα ταῦτ᾿ ἐν εὐχερεῖ   875
ἔθου, βοῆς τε καὶ δυσοσμίας γέμων.

74

In sickness all men's slumber
is not real sleep—it has keen eyes.
I think you should use the utmost care,
doing everything within your power,
and take that bow—a major prize.   [850]
Take it without alerting him.
If you hold to what you intend for him—
and you know clearly what I mean—
then there are surely going to be
some desperate problems facing us,
which a shrewd man could well foresee.[20]
Now, lad, a fair wind blows you on your course,
this man's eyes are closed, his weapon's gone,
and he's stretched out in a dark sleep—
and in this heat a man sleeps soundly.
He can't control his hands or feet,   [860]
like someone lying with Hades.
So think if what you've talked about
is practical. Consider that. My boy,
as far as I can grasp what's happening,
the finest action is the one
where there's nothing to fear.

NEOPTOLEMUS

Keep quiet, I tell you. Don't lose your wits.
He's opening his eyes—raising his head.

[Philoctetes wakes up and struggles to stand and look around him]

PHILOCTETES

Ah, to sleep and then to see the daylight
and friendly people watching out for me,
a sight beyond my fondest hopes! My boy,
I never would have thought you'd do this—
remain here with such sympathy and wait   [870]
to help me until my fit was over.
Those fine generals, the sons of Atreus,
you can be sure, would not have done that,
not so readily. But your nature, lad,
is good—you've got a noble ancestry.
So you bore all these troubles easily,
the cries of pain and the appalling stench.

καὶ νῦν ἐπειδὴ τοῦδε τοῦ κακοῦ δοκεῖ
λήθη τις εἶναι κἀνάπαυλα δή, τέκνον,
σύ μ᾽ αὐτὸς ἆρον, σύ με κατάστησον, τέκνον,
ἵν᾽, ἡνίκ᾽ ἂν κόπος μ᾽ ἀπαλλάξῃ ποτέ,   880
ὁρμώμεθ᾽ ἐς ναῦν μηδ᾽ ἐπίσχωμεν τὸ πλεῖν.

ΝΕΟΠΤΟΛΕΜΟΣ
ἀλλ᾽ ἥδομαι μέν σ᾽ εἰσιδὼν παρ᾽ ἐλπίδα
ἀνώδυνον βλέποντα κἀμπνέοντ᾽ ἔτι·
ὡς οὐκέτ᾽ ὄντος γὰρ τὰ συμβόλαιά σου
πρὸς τὰς παρούσας ξυμφορὰς ἐφαίνετο.   885
νῦν δ᾽ αἶρε σαυτόν· εἰ δέ σοι μᾶλλον φίλον,
οἴσουσί σ᾽ οἵδε· τοῦ πόνου γὰρ οὐκ ὄκνος,
ἐπείπερ οὕτω σοί τ᾽ ἔδοξ᾽ ἐμοί τε δρᾶν.

ΦΙΛΟΚΤΗΤΗΣ
αἰνῶ τάδ᾽, ὦ παῖ, καί μ᾽ ἔπαιρ᾽, ὥσπερ νοεῖς·
τούτους δ᾽ ἔασον, μὴ βαρυνθῶσιν κακῇ   890
ὀσμῇ πρὸ τοῦ δέοντος· οὑπὶ νηὶ γὰρ
ἅλις πόνος τούτοισι συνναίειν ἐμοί.

ΝΕΟΠΤΟΛΕΜΟΣ
ἔσται τάδ᾽· ἀλλ᾽ ἴστω τε καὐτὸς ἀντέχου.

ΦΙΛΟΚΤΗΤΗΣ
θάρσει· τό τοι σύνηθες ὀρθώσει μ᾽ ἔθος.

ΝΕΟΠΤΟΛΕΜΟΣ
παπαῖ· τί δῆτ᾽ ἂν δρῷμ᾽ ἐγὼ τοὐνθένδε γε;   895

ΦΙΛΟΚΤΗΤΗΣ
τί δ᾽ ἔστιν, ὦ παῖ; ποῖ ποτ᾽ ἐξέβης λόγῳ;

ΝΕΟΠΤΟΛΕΜΟΣ
οὐκ οἶδ᾽ ὅποι χρὴ τἄπορον τρέπειν ἔπος.

ΦΙΛΟΚΤΗΤΗΣ
ἀπορεῖς δὲ τοῦ σύ; μὴ λέγ᾽, ὦ τέκνον, τάδε.

And now it looks as if I can forget
this illness and rest awhile. So, my boy,
lift me up. Help me to my feet, lad.
When I recover from this dizziness,   [880]
we'll go to the ship and sail without delay.

NEOPTOLEMUS

I'm glad to see you're still alive, breathing
without that pain. What I was expecting
was something else—in your endless suffering
your symptoms made you look as if you'd died.
Now you should get up. Or, if you prefer,
these men will carry you. It's no trouble,
since you and I agree what we're to do.

PHILOCTETES

Thanks, my lad. Why not help me up yourself,
as you were going to? Leave the men alone,   [890]
so they don't get upset by the foul smell
before they have to. It will be hard enough
for them to be on board the ship with me.

NEOPTOLEMUS

All right, then. I'll take hold of you. Stand up.

PHILOCTETES

Don't worry. I'll do what I always do
to get up on my feet.

*[PHILOCTETES struggles with great difficulty to stand up.
NEOPTOLEMUS watches him]*

NEOPTOLEMUS

                        This is dreadful—
what am I supposed to do at this point?

PHILOCTETES

What is it, lad? Those words sound out of place.

NEOPTOLEMUS

I don't know how I need to frame my words . . .
It's so confusing . . .

PHILOCTETES

                        You're confused?
No, no, my boy, don't say such things.

Sophocles

ΝΕΟΠΤΟΛΕΜΟΣ

ἀλλ᾽ ἐνθάδ᾽ ἤδη τοῦδε τοῦ πάθους κυρῶ.

ΦΙΛΟΚΤΗΤΗΣ

οὐ δή σε δυσχέρεια τοῦ νοσήματος   900
ἔπεισεν ὥστε μή μ᾽ ἄγειν ναύτην ἔτι;

ΝΕΟΠΤΟΛΕΜΟΣ

ἅπαντα δυσχέρεια, τὴν αὑτοῦ φύσιν
ὅταν λιπών τις δρᾷ τὰ μὴ προσεικότα.

ΦΙΛΟΚΤΗΤΗΣ

ἀλλ᾽ οὐδὲν ἔξω τοῦ φυτεύσαντος σύ γε
δρᾷς οὐδὲ φωνεῖς, ἐσθλὸν ἄνδρ᾽ ἐπωφελῶν.   905

ΝΕΟΠΤΟΛΕΜΟΣ

αἰσχρὸς φανοῦμαι· τοῦτ᾽ ἀνιῶμαι πάλαι.

ΦΙΛΟΚΤΗΤΗΣ

οὔκουν ἐν οἷς γε δρᾷς· ἐν οἷς δ᾽ αὐδᾷς ὀκνῶ.

ΝΕΟΠΤΟΛΕΜΟΣ

ὦ Ζεῦ, τί δράσω; δεύτερον ληφθῶ κακός,
κρύπτων θ᾽ ἃ μὴ δεῖ καὶ λέγων αἴσχιστ᾽ ἐπῶν;

ΦΙΛΟΚΤΗΤΗΣ

ἀνὴρ ὅδ᾽, εἰ μὴ ᾽γὼ κακὸς γνώμων ἔφυν,   910
προδούς μ᾽ ἔοικε κἀκλιπὼν τὸν πλοῦν στελεῖν.

ΝΕΟΠΤΟΛΕΜΟΣ

λιπὼν μὲν οὐκ ἔγωγε· λυπηρῶς δὲ μὴ
πέμπω σε μᾶλλον, τοῦτ᾽ ἀνιῶμαι πάλαι.

ΦΙΛΟΚΤΗΤΗΣ

τί ποτε λέγεις, ὦ τέκνον; ὡς οὐ μανθάνω.

78

NEOPTOLEMUS
The position I'm in . . . it makes me feel like that.

PHILOCTETES
The disgust you feel about my sickness—   [900]
surely that feeling has not persuaded you
not to take me on your ship?

NEOPTOLEMUS
                                        When a man
abandons his own nature and then acts
against his character, all things are dreadful.

PHILOCTETES
But you, at least, by helping a good man
have not been doing or saying anything
your father wouldn't have done.

NEOPTOLEMUS
                                        I'll be dishonored—
that's the thought that keeps tormenting me.

PHILOCTETES
No, not because of what you're doing now.
But the way you're talking has me worried.

NEOPTOLEMUS
O Zeus, what do I do? Will I be disgraced
twice over—hiding what I should not hide
and forfeiting my honour with my words?

PHILOCTETES
Unless I've judged this situation badly,   [910]
this man's intending to betray me—
he'll leave me here and sail away.

NEOPTOLEMUS
                                        No!
I won't abandon you. I'll take you with me,
but you'll really find the trip distressing.
All this time that's what's been troubling me.

PHILOCTETES
What do you mean, my boy? I do not understand.

ΝΕΟΠΤΟΛΕΜΟΣ
οὐδέν σε κρύψω· δεῖ γὰρ ἐς Τροίαν σε πλεῖν   915
πρὸς τοὺς Ἀχαιοὺς καὶ τὸν Ἀτρειδῶν στόλον.

ΦΙΛΟΚΤΗΤΗΣ
οἴμοι, τί εἶπας;

ΝΕΟΠΤΟΛΕΜΟΣ
     μὴ στέναζε, πρὶν μάθῃς.

ΦΙΛΟΚΤΗΤΗΣ
ποῖον μάθημα; τί με νοεῖς δρᾶσαί ποτε;

ΝΕΟΠΤΟΛΕΜΟΣ
σῶσαι κακοῦ μὲν πρῶτα τοῦδ᾽, ἔπειτα δὲ
ξὺν σοὶ τὰ Τροίας πεδία πορθῆσαι μολών.   920

ΦΙΛΟΚΤΗΤΗΣ
καὶ ταῦτ᾽ ἀληθῆ δρᾶν νοεῖς;

ΝΕΟΠΤΟΛΕΜΟΣ
     πολλὴ κρατεῖ
τούτων ἀνάγκη, καὶ σὺ μὴ θυμοῦ κλύων.

ΦΙΛΟΚΤΗΤΗΣ
ἀπόλωλα τλήμων, προδέδομαι. τί μ᾽, ὦ ξένε,
δέδρακας; ἀπόδος ὡς τάχος τὰ τόξα μοι.

ΝΕΟΠΤΟΛΕΜΟΣ
ἀλλ᾽ οὐχ οἷόν τε· τῶν γὰρ ἐν τέλει κλύειν   925
τό τ᾽ ἔνδικόν με καὶ τὸ συμφέρον ποεῖ.

ΦΙΛΟΚΤΗΤΗΣ
ὦ πῦρ σὺ καὶ πᾶν δεῖμα καὶ πανουργίας
δεινῆς τέχνημ᾽ ἔχθιστον, οἷά μ᾽ εἰργάσω,
οἷ᾽ ἠπάτηκας· οὐδ᾽ ἐπαισχύνει μ᾽ ὁρῶν
τὸν προστρόπαιον, τὸν ἱκέτην, ὦ σχέτλιε;   930

NEOPTOLEMUS
    I won't conceal a thing. You must sail to Troy,
    back to the Achaeans and the army
    led by those sons of Atreus.

PHILOCTETES
                                    O no!
    What are you saying?

NEOPTOLEMUS
                        Don't start wailing,
    not until you learn what it's about.

PHILOCTETES
    What's there to learn? What are you doing with me?

NEOPTOLEMUS
    First, I'm saving you from this awful place.
    And then I'm going with you to plunder Troy.   [920]

PHILOCTETES
    And that is what you really mean to do?

NEOPTOLEMUS
    There's a powerful necessity at work
    controlling these events. Keep your temper
    when you hear the story.

PHILOCTETES
                                I'm done for . . .
    betrayed . . . this is appalling! You stranger,
    why have you done this to me? My bow—
    give it back to me right now!

NEOPTOLEMUS
                            I can't do that.
    Both my duty and my own self-interest
    compel me to obey those in command.

PHILOCTETES
    You destructive fire . . . you total monster . . .
    you hateful masterpiece of fearful treachery—
    what you've done to me, how you've betrayed me!
    Aren't you ashamed to look at me, a man
    who was your suppliant, who begged your mercy?   [930]

81

Sophocles

ἀπεστέρηκας τὸν βίον τὰ τόξ᾽ ἑλών.
ἀπόδος, ἱκνοῦμαί σ᾽, ἀπόδος, ἱκετεύω, τέκνον·
πρὸς θεῶν πατρῴων, τὸν βίον με μὴ ἀφέλῃ.
ὤμοι τάλας. ἀλλ᾽ οὐδὲ προσφωνεῖ μ᾽ ἔτι,
ἀλλ᾽ ὡς μεθήσων μήποθ᾽, ὧδ᾽ ὁρᾷ πάλιν.   935
ὦ λιμένες, ὦ προβλῆτες, ὦ ξυνουσίαι
θηρῶν ὀρείων, ὦ καταρρῶγες πέτραι,
ὑμῖν τάδ᾽, οὐ γὰρ ἄλλον οἶδ᾽ ὅτῳ λέγω,
ἀνακλαίομαι παροῦσι τοῖς εἰωθόσιν,
οἷ᾽ ἔργ᾽ ὁ παῖς μ᾽ ἔδρασεν οὑξ Ἀχιλλέως·   940
ὀμόσας ἀπάξειν οἴκαδ᾽, ἐς Τροίαν μ᾽ ἄγει·
προσθείς τε χεῖρα δεξιάν, τὰ τόξα μου
ἱερὰ λαβὼν τοῦ Ζηνὸς Ἡρακλέους ἔχει,
καὶ τοῖσιν Ἀργείοισι φήνασθαι θέλει·
ὡς ἄνδρ᾽ ἑλὼν ἰσχυρόν ἐκ βίας μ᾽ ἄγει,   945
κοὐκ οἶδ᾽ ἐναίρων νεκρὸν ἢ καπνοῦ σκιάν,
εἴδωλον ἄλλως· οὐ γὰρ ἂν σθένοντά γε
εἷλέν μ᾽· ἐπεὶ οὐδ᾽ ἂν ὧδ᾽ ἔχοντ᾽, εἰ μὴ δόλῳ.
νῦν δ᾽ ἠπάτημαι δύσμορος. τί χρή με δρᾶν;
ἀλλ᾽ ἀπόδος, ἀλλὰ νῦν ἔτ᾽ ἐν σαυτῷ γενοῦ.   950
τί φῄς; σιωπᾷς; οὐδέν εἰμ᾽ ὁ δύσμορος.
ὦ σχῆμα πέτρας δίπυλον, αὖθις αὖ πάλιν
εἴσειμι πρὸς σὲ ψιλός, οὐκ ἔχων τροφήν·
ἀλλ᾽ αὐανοῦμαι τῷδ᾽ ἐν αὐλίῳ μόνος,
οὐ πτηνὸν ὄρνιν οὐδὲ θῆρ᾽ ὀρειβάτην   955
τόξοις ἐναίρων τοισίδ᾽, ἀλλ᾽ αὐτὸς τάλας
θανὼν παρέξω δαῖθ᾽ ὑφ᾽ ὧν ἐφερβόμην,
καί μ᾽ οὓς ἐθήρων πρόσθε θηράσουσι νῦν·
φόνον φόνου δὲ ῥύσιον τίσω τάλας

You wretch! When you deprive me of my bow,
you take away my life. So hand it back.
I'm begging you. Please, my lad, return it.
By your fathers' gods, don't rob me of my life!

[NEOPTOLEMUS remains silent and cannot look at PHILOCTETES]

This is atrocious! He's not speaking to me.
He won't even look me in the eye,
as if he'll never give me back my bow.
O you bays and headlands, you mountain beasts,
who've been part of my life, you jagged rocks,
to you I call—there's no one else to hear me.
So to you, my customary companions,
I cry out what this boy has done to me,   [940]
Achilles' son, who made me a promise
he'd take me home and who now leads me off
to Troy. With his right hand he pledged his word,
then took my bow and keeps it for himself,
the sacred bow of Hercules, Zeus' son,
which he desires to show off to the Argives.
He's taking me by force, as if I were
some mighty warrior—he doesn't realize
he's destroying a corpse, a smoky shadow,
no more than a mere ghost. If I were strong,
he'd not have captured me—even as it is,
with me in this condition, he'd not prevail
except by trickery. It's my harsh fate.
My hopes have been betrayed. What should I do?
Give back the bow. Return to who you are,   [950]
to your true character. What do you say?
You're silent, and I'm a wretched nothing!
I'll go back once again to you, my rock
with your two entrances, but unarmed now,
without a way to get my nourishment.
And in this cave I'll waste away alone,
unable to bring down with my arrows
birds on the wing or beasts that roam the hills.
Instead I'll die a miserable death.
Now I'm a feast for those I used to feed on,
the prey of those I hunted down before.
I'll pay a full reprisal with my life,
my dismal life, for those whose lives I took,

Sophocles

πρὸς τοῦ δοκοῦντος οὐδὲν εἰδέναι κακόν.　960
ὄλοιο—μή πω, πρὶν μάθοιμ᾽ εἰ καὶ πάλιν
γνώμην μετοίσεις· εἰ δὲ μή, θάνοις κακῶς.

ΧΟΡΟΣ

τί δρῶμεν; ἐν σοὶ καὶ τὸ πλεῖν ἡμᾶς, ἄναξ,
ἤδη ᾽στὶ καὶ τοῖς τοῦδε προσχωρεῖν λόγοις.

ΝΕΟΠΤΟΛΕΜΟΣ

ἐμοὶ μὲν οἶκτος δεινὸς ἐμπέπτωκέ τις　965
τοῦδ᾽ ἀνδρὸς οὐ νῦν πρῶτον, ἀλλὰ καὶ πάλαι.

ΦΙΛΟΚΤΗΤΗΣ

ἐλέησον, ὦ παῖ, πρὸς θεῶν, καὶ μὴ παρῇς
σαυτοῦ βροτοῖς ὄνειδος, ἐκκλέψας ἐμέ.

ΝΕΟΠΤΟΛΕΜΟΣ

οἴμοι, τί δράσω; μή ποτ᾽ ὤφελον λιπεῖν
τὴν Σκῦρον· οὕτω τοῖς παροῦσιν ἄχθομαι.　970

ΦΙΛΟΚΤΗΤΗΣ

οὐκ εἶ κακὸς σύ, πρὸς κακῶν δ᾽ ἀνδρῶν μαθὼν
ἔοικας ἥκειν αἰσχρά· νῦν δ᾽ ἄλλοισι δοὺς
οἷς εἰκὸς ἔκπλει, τἀμά μοι μεθεὶς ὅπλα.

ΝΕΟΠΤΟΛΕΜΟΣ

τί δρῶμεν, ἄνδρες;

ΟΔΥΣΣΕΥΣ

　　　　　ὦ κάκιστ᾽ ἀνδρῶν, τί δρᾷς;
οὐκ εἶ μεθεὶς τὰ τόξα ταῦτ᾽ ἐμοὶ πάλιν;　975

ΦΙΛΟΚΤΗΤΗΣ

οἴμοι, τίς ἀνήρ; ἆρ᾽ Ὀδυσσέως κλύω;

84

thanks to a man who looked as if he had   [960]
no sense of evil. May you perish, too!
But no, not quite yet, not before I see
if you will change your mind again. If not,
I hope you die a truly wretched death!

CHORUS
What shall we do? It's up to you, my king,
whether we sail off now or else comply
with what he's asking.

NEOPTOLEMUS
                          Pity for this man,
a dreadful pity, has come over me,
and it's not something new. No. I've felt it
for a long time now.

PHILOCTETES
                          By the gods, my boy,
have mercy on me. Don't give people cause
to criticize you for deceiving me.

NEOPTOLEMUS
No, not that! What am I going to do?
I wish I'd never sailed away from Scyros!   [970]
What's going on here is just too painful.

PHILOCTETES
You're not an evil man, but it seems to me
you came here after learning shameful things
from wicked men. Leave bad deeds to others,
those fit to act that way, and sail from here.
But first give me my weapon.

NEOPTOLEMUS
                          You men,
what shall we do?

*[Enter ODYSSEUS with a small escort of armed sailors. PHILOCTETES
does see him immediately]*

ODYSSEUS
                          What are you doing,
you traitor? Come back here. Give me that bow.

PHILOCTETES
Who's that? Do I hear Odysseus' voice?

85

Sophocles

ΟΔΥΣΣΕΥΣ
Ὀδυσσέως, σάφ᾽ ἴσθ᾽, ἐμοῦ γ᾽, ὃν εἰσορᾷς.

ΦΙΛΟΚΤΗΤΗΣ
οἴμοι· πέπραμαι κἀπόλωλ᾽· ὅδ᾽ ἦν ἄρα
ὁ ξυλλαβών με κἀπονοσφίσας ὅπλων.

ΟΔΥΣΣΕΥΣ
ἐγώ, σάφ᾽ ἴσθ᾽, οὐκ ἄλλος· ὁμολογῶ τάδε.　　　　980

ΦΙΛΟΚΤΗΤΗΣ
ἀπόδος, ἄφες μοι, παῖ, τὰ τόξα.

ΟΔΥΣΣΕΥΣ
　　　　　　　　　τοῦτο μέν,
οὐδ᾽ ἢν θέλῃ, δράσει ποτ᾽· ἀλλὰ καὶ σὲ δεῖ
στείχειν ἅμ᾽ αὐτοῖς, ἢ βίᾳ στελοῦσί σε.

ΦΙΛΟΚΤΗΤΗΣ
ἔμ᾽, ὦ κακῶν κάκιστε καὶ τολμήσατε,
οἵδ᾽ ἐκ βίας ἄξουσιν;　　　　985

ΟΔΥΣΣΕΥΣ
　　　　　　　ἢν μὴ ἕρπῃς ἑκών.

ΦΙΛΟΚΤΗΤΗΣ
ὦ Λημνία χθὼν καὶ τὸ παγκρατὲς σέλας
Ἡφαιστότευκτον, ταῦτα δῆτ᾽ ἀνασχετά,
εἴ μ᾽ οὗτος ἐκ τῶν σῶν ἀπάξεται βίᾳ;

ΟΔΥΣΣΕΥΣ
Ζεύς ἐσθ᾽, ἵν᾽ εἰδῇς, Ζεύς, ὁ τῆσδε γῆς κρατῶν,
Ζεύς, ᾧ δέδοκται ταῦθ᾽· ὑπηρετῶ δ᾽ ἐγώ.　　　　990

ΦΙΛΟΚΤΗΤΗΣ
ὦ μῖσος, οἷα κἀξανευρίσκεις λέγειν·
θεοὺς προτείνων τοὺς θεοὺς ψευδεῖς τίθης.

86

ODYSSEUS *[stepping forward]*
> Yes, it is Odysseus. Now you can grasp
> the way things are. I'm here. See for yourself.

PHILOCTETES
> Alas, I've been betrayed. I'm being destroyed.
> So he's the one who really caught me out
> and stole my weapons.

ODYSSEUS
>   That right. It's was me   [980]
> and no one else. I will acknowledge that.

PHILOCTETES
> Give me the bow, boy. Hand it over.

ODYSSEUS
> He won't do it, even if he wants to.
> No. You've got to come along with me.
> If not, these men will take you off by force.

PHILOCTETES
> Of all evil men, you are the nastiest—
> and boldest, too. They'll take me in by force?

ODYSSEUS
> Yes, unless you come of your own free will.

PHILOCTETES
> O Lemnos and you all-powerful flames
> lit by Hephaestus, can you endure this—
> that this man will compel me now to leave?

ODYSSEUS
> I tell you it's Zeus who rules this country.
> Yes, Zeus. And this has been ordained by Zeus.   [990]
> I am his servant.

PHILOCTETES
>   You despicable man,
> you just invent the things you wish to say,
> and by making claims about the gods,
> you turn them into liars.

Sophocles

ΟΔΥΣΣΕΥΣ

οὔκ, ἀλλ' ἀληθεῖς· ἡ δ' ὁδὸς πορευτέα.

ΦΙΛΟΚΤΗΤΗΣ

οὔ φημ'.

ΟΔΥΣΣΕΥΣ

ἐγὼ δέ φημι. πειστέον τάδε.

ΦΙΛΟΚΤΗΤΗΣ

οἴμοι τάλας. ἡμᾶς μὲν ὡς δούλους σαφῶς   995
πατὴρ ἄρ' ἐξέφυσεν οὐδ' ἐλευθέρους.

ΟΔΥΣΣΕΥΣ

οὔκ, ἀλλ' ὁμοίους τοῖς ἀρίστοισιν, μεθ' ὧν
Τροίαν σ' ἑλεῖν δεῖ καὶ κατασκάψαι βίᾳ.

ΦΙΛΟΚΤΗΤΗΣ

οὐδέποτέ γ'· οὐδ' ἢν χρῇ με πᾶν παθεῖν κακόν,
ἕως ἂν ᾖ μοι γῆς τόδ' αἰπεινὸν βάθρον.   1000

ΟΔΥΣΣΕΥΣ

τί δ' ἐργασείεις;

ΦΙΛΟΚΤΗΤΗΣ

κρᾶτ' ἐμὸν τόδ' αὐτίκα
πέτρᾳ πέτρας ἄνωθεν αἱμάξω πεσών.

ΟΔΥΣΣΕΥΣ

ξυλλάβετον αὐτόν· μὴ 'πὶ τῷδ' ἔστω τάδε.

ΦΙΛΟΚΤΗΤΗΣ

ὦ χεῖρες, οἷα πάσχετ' ἐν χρείᾳ φίλης
νευρᾶς, ὑπ' ἀνδρὸς τοῦδε συνθηρώμεναι.   1005
ὦ μηδὲν ὑγιὲς μηδ' ἐλεύθερον φρονῶν,

ODYSSEUS
                              No, I don't.
    They speak the truth. We have to go.

PHILOCTETES
                                    I won't.

ODYSSEUS
    But I say you will. You have to obey.

PHILOCTETES
    This is all so shameful—it's clear enough
    my father conceived in me a slave
    and no free man.

ODYSSEUS
                  You're wrong. He made a man
    to be just like the finest warriors
    with whom you're going to capture Troy by force
    and then destroy it.

PHILOCTETES
                      I'll never do it,
    not even if I have to undergo
    every kind of torment, not while I stand
    with these steep island rocks below me.   [1000]

ODYSSEUS
                  What will you do?

PHILOCTETES
    I'll throw myself directly from this cliff
    and smash my head in on the stone down there.

ODYSSEUS *[to his attendants]*
    Grab him, you two! Don't let him do that!

[The two sailors rush up and grab Philoctetes by his arms]

PHILOCTETES
    O my arms, what suffering you must bear
    because you lack that bow you cherish so!
    Now you've become a tied-up captive beast,
    thanks to this man. And you, who cannot think
    a healthy thought that suits a man who's free,

οἷ᾽ αὖ μ᾽ ὑπῆλθες, ὥς μ᾽ ἐθηράσω, λαβὼν
πρόβλημα σαυτοῦ παῖδα τόνδ᾽ ἀγνῶτ᾽ ἐμοί,
ἀνάξιον μὲν σοῦ, κατάξιον δ᾽ ἐμοῦ,
ὃς οὐδὲν ᾔδει πλὴν τὸ προσταχθὲν ποεῖν,   1010
δῆλος δὲ καὶ νῦν ἐστιν ἀλγεινῶς φέρων
οἷς τ᾽ αὐτὸς ἐξήμαρτεν οἷς τ᾽ ἐγὼ 'παθον.
ἀλλ᾽ ἡ κακὴ σὴ διὰ μυχῶν βλέπουσ᾽ ἀεὶ
ψυχή νιν ἀφυῆ τ᾽ ὄντα κοὐ θέλονθ᾽ ὅμως
εὖ προυδίδαξεν ἐν κακοῖς εἶναι σοφόν.   1015
καὶ νῦν ἔμ᾽, ὦ δύστηνε, συνδήσας νοεῖς
ἄγειν ἀπ᾽ ἀκτῆς τῆσδ᾽, ἐν ᾗ με προυβάλου
ἄφιλον ἔρημον ἄπολιν, ἐν ζῶσιν νεκρόν.
φεῦ.
ὄλοιο· καί σοι πολλάκις τόδ᾽ ηὐξάμην.
ἀλλ᾽ οὐ γὰρ οὐδὲν θεοὶ νέμουσιν ἡδύ μοι,   1020
σὺ μὲν γέγηθας ζῶν, ἐγὼ δ᾽ ἀλγύνομαι
τοῦτ᾽ αὖθ᾽, ὅτι ζῶ σὺν κακοῖς πολλοῖς τάλας,
γελώμενος πρὸς σοῦ τε καὶ τῶν Ἀτρέως
διπλῶν στρατηγῶν, οἷς σὺ ταῦθ᾽ ὑπηρετεῖς.
καίτοι σὺ μὲν κλοπῇ τε κἀνάγκῃ ζυγεὶς   1025
ἔπλεις ἅμ᾽ αὐτοῖς, ἐμὲ δὲ τὸν πανάθλιον,
ἑκόντα πλεύσανθ᾽ ἑπτὰ ναυσὶ ναυβάτην,
ἄτιμον ἔβαλον, ὡς σὺ φής, κεῖνοι δὲ σέ.
καὶ νῦν τί μ᾽ ἄγετε; τί μ᾽ ἀπάγεσθε; τοῦ χάριν;
ὃς οὐδέν εἰμι καὶ τέθνηχ᾽ ὑμῖν πάλαι.   1030
πῶς, ὦ θεοῖς ἔχθιστε, νῦν οὐκ εἰμί σοι
χωλός, δυσώδης; πῶς θεοῖς ἔξεσθ᾽, ὁμοῦ
πλεύσαντος αἴθειν ἱερά; πῶς σπένδειν ἔτι;
αὕτη γὰρ ἦν σοι πρόφασις ἐκβαλεῖν ἐμέ.
κακῶς ὄλοισθ᾽· ὀλεῖσθε δ᾽ ἠδικηκότες   1035

you've sneaked up and snagged me once again,
using this young lad, whom I didn't know,
to be your screen. Though he's too good for you,
he's someone worthy of my company—
he only thought of following his orders,   [1010]
and he's already showing his remorse
for mistakes he's made and what I've suffered.
Your vicious spirit, always peering out
from secret hiding places, trained him well
to be adept in acting with deceit,
though that was not his nature or his wish.
And now, you wretch, you mean to tie me up
and take me from the very shore where once
you left me by myself—without a friend,
without a city—for all living men
nothing but a corpse. Ah, I hope you die!
I've often prayed that death would come for you.
But gods have granted nothing sweet to me,   [1020]
so you remain alive and keep on laughing,
while I am suffering pain and living on
with so much agony, a laughing stock
for you and those two sons of Atreus,
those generals you serve in doing this,
although you only sailed away with them
once you'd been forced under their yoke by tricks
and by compulsion. But I sailed with them
of my own free will, bringing seven ships.[21]
A complete disaster! They threw me out,
off the ship, like someone with no honour.
You say they did it. They say it was you.
So why are you now taking me away?
Why am I going with you? What's the reason?
I'm nothing, and, so far as you're concerned,   [1030]
for a long time I've been dead. How is it,
you creature whom the gods despise, that now
you do not view me as a stinking cripple?
If I sail with you, how will you then
make holy sacrifices anymore?
Or pour libations? That was your excuse
for throwing me ashore back then. I hope
you die a disgusting death! And you will,

Sophocles

τὸν ἄνδρα τόνδε, θεοῖσιν εἰ δίκης μέλει.
ἔξοιδα δ' ὡς μέλει γ'· ἐπεὶ οὔποτ' ἂν στόλον
ἐπλεύσατ' ἂν τόνδ' εἵνεκ' ἀνδρὸς ἀθλίου,
εἰ μή τι κέντρον θεῖον ἦγ' ὑμᾶς ἐμοῦ.
ἀλλ', ὦ πατρῷα γῆ θεοί τ' ἐπόψιοι,   1040
τίσασθε τίσασθ' ἀλλὰ τῷ χρόνῳ ποτὲ
ξύμπαντας αὐτούς, εἴ τι κἄμ' οἰκτίρετε·
ὡς ζῶ μὲν οἰκτρῶς, εἰ δ' ἴδοιμ' ὀλωλότας
τούτους, δοκοῖμ' ἂν τῆς νόσου πεφευγέναι.

ΧΟΡΟΣ
βαρύς τε καὶ βαρεῖαν ὁ ξένος φάτιν   1045
τήνδ' εἶπ', Ὀδυσσεῦ, κοὐχ ὑπείκουσαν κακοῖς.

ΟΔΥΣΣΕΥΣ
πόλλ' ἂν λέγειν ἔχοιμι πρὸς τὰ τοῦδ' ἔπη,
εἴ μοι παρείκοι· νῦν δ' ἑνὸς κρατῶ λόγου.
οὗ γὰρ τοιούτων δεῖ, τοιοῦτός εἰμ' ἐγώ·
χὤπου δικαίων κἀγαθῶν ἀνδρῶν κρίσις,   1050
οὐκ ἂν λάβοις μου μᾶλλον οὐδέν' εὐσεβῆ.
νικᾶν γε μέντοι πανταχοῦ χρῄζων ἔφυν,
πλὴν εἰς σέ· νῦν δὲ σοί γ' ἑκὼν ἐκστήσομαι.
ἄφετε γὰρ αὐτὸν μηδὲ προσψαύσητ' ἔτι·
ἐᾶτε μίμνειν. οὐδὲ σοῦ προσχρῄζομεν,   1055
τά γ' ὅπλ' ἔχοντες ταῦτ', ἐπεὶ πάρεστι μὲν
Τεῦκρος παρ' ἡμῖν, τήνδ' ἐπιστήμην ἔχων,
ἐγώ θ', ὃς οἶμαι σοῦ κάκιον οὐδὲν ἂν
τούτων κρατύνειν, μηδ' ἐπιθύνειν χερί.
τί δῆτα σοῦ δεῖ; χαῖρε τὴν Λῆμνον πατῶν·   1060
ἡμεῖς δ' ἴωμεν, καὶ τάχ' ἂν τὸ σὸν γέρας
τιμὴν ἐμοὶ νείμειεν, ἣν σὲ χρῆν ἔχειν.

ΦΙΛΟΚΤΗΤΗΣ
οἴμοι· τί δράσω δύσμορος; σὺ τοῖς ἐμοῖς
ὅπλοισι κοσμηθεὶς ἐν Ἀργείοις φανεῖ;

92

for the evil things you've done to hurt me,
if the gods have any sense of justice.
I know they are concerned about these things.
You never would have sailed on such a trip,
all for the sake of such a wretched man,
unless some god-sent spur was pricking you
to come and get me. O land of my fathers,   [1040]
you gods who gaze on what we mortals do,
if you pity me, bring on your vengeance,
and, after these long years, pay them all back.
My life deserves your pity. If I could see
them killed, I'd think I was no longer sick.

CHORUS

What the stranger said was harsh, Odysseus—
his troubles have not eased his bitterness.

ODYSSEUS

I could go on and answer him at length,
if I had time. There's only one thing now
I'll say to him. I'm the kind of man
who adapts himself to each occasion.
So, faced with being judged by good, fair men,   [1050]
you'd find no one more pious than myself.
By nature I'm a man who needs to win
in everything—however, not with you.
So now I'll happily defer to you.
Let him go. There's no longer any need
for you to hold him. Let him remain here.
We have Teucer with us, a skilled archer.[22]
So am I, and I believe it's possible
for me to use this bow no worse than you—
my hand can aim it just as well as yours.
So why do we need you? Enjoy yourself   [1060]
strolling here on Lemnos. We'll be on our way.
Your prize may quickly bring me honours
which should belong to you.

PHILOCTETES

No, not that!
You are going to march among the Argives
equipped with weapons which belong to me?

93

Sophocles

ΟΔΥΣΣΕΥΣ

μή μ᾽ ἀντιφώνει μηδέν, ὡς στείχοντα δή.　　　1065

ΦΙΛΟΚΤΗΤΗΣ

ὦ σπέρμ᾽ Ἀχιλλέως, οὐδὲ σοῦ φωνῆς ἔτι
γενήσομαι προσφθεγκτός, ἀλλ᾽ οὕτως ἄπει;

ΟΔΥΣΣΕΥΣ

χώρει σύ· μὴ πρόσλευσσε, γενναῖός περ ὤν,
ἡμῶν ὅπως μὴ τὴν τύχην διαφθερεῖς.

ΦΙΛΟΚΤΗΤΗΣ

ἦ καὶ πρὸς ὑμῶν ὧδ᾽ ἔρημος, ὦ ξένοι,　　　1070
λειφθήσομαι δὴ κοὐκ ἐποικτερεῖτέ με;

ΧΟΡΟΣ

ὅδ᾽ ἐστὶν ἡμῶν ναυκράτωρ ὁ παῖς· ὅσ᾽ ἂν
οὗτος λέγῃ σοι, ταῦτά σοι χἠμεῖς φαμέν.

ΝΕΟΠΤΟΛΕΜΟΣ

ἀκούσομαι μὲν ὡς ἔφυν οἴκτου πλέως
πρὸς τοῦδ᾽· ὅμως δὲ μείνατ᾽, εἰ τούτῳ δοκεῖ,　　　1075
χρόνον τοσοῦτον, εἰς ὅσον τά τ᾽ ἐκ νεὼς
στείλωσι ναῦται καὶ θεοῖς εὐξώμεθα.
χοὗτος τάχ᾽ ἂν φρόνησιν ἐν τούτῳ λάβοι
λῴω τιν᾽ ἡμῖν. νὼ μὲν οὖν ὁρμώμεθον,
ὑμεῖς δ᾽, ὅταν καλῶμεν, ὁρμᾶσθαι ταχεῖς.　　　1080

ΦΙΛΟΚΤΗΤΗΣ

ὦ κοίλας πέτρας γύαλον
θερμὸν καὶ παγετῶδες, ὥς σ᾽ οὐκ ἔμελλον ἄρ᾽, ὦ τάλας,
λείψειν οὐδέποτ᾽, ἀλλά μοι καὶ θνῄσκοντι συνείσει.
ὤμοι μοί μοι.　　　1086
ὦ πληρέστατον αὔλιον
λύπας τᾶς ἀπ᾽ ἐμοῦ τάλαν,
τίπτ᾽ αὖ μοι τὸ κατ᾽ ἆμαρ
ἔσται; τοῦ ποτε τεύξομαι　　　1090
σιτονόμου μέλεος πόθεν ἐλπίδος;

94

ODYSSEUS
Don't argue with me anymore. I'm going.

PHILOCTETES
Son of Achilles, am I going to hear
your voice say anything to me? Are you
about to leave without another word?

ODYSSEUS *[to Neoptolemus]*
Move on. Don't look at him. You may well be
a noble man, but don't ruin our good luck.

PHILOCTETES *[to the Chorus]*
And you, my guests, will you leave me like this   [1070]
and not feel pity?

CHORUS
                              The boy commands our ship.
What he says to you—that's what we say, as well.

NEOPTOLEMUS *[to the Chorus]*
Odysseus will say I am too sensitive—
but you stay here, if that's all right with him,
until the sailors have prepared the ship
and we have offered prayers up to the gods.
Philoctetes may quickly change his mind
and soon think better of us. But we two
are leaving now. When we call for you,   [1080]
make sure you leave from here at once.

[Neoptolemus and Odysseus leave]

PHILOCTETES *[addressing his cave]*
You cavern in this hollow rock,
always freezing cold or else too hot.
In my illness, then, it does seem true,
it's never been my fate to leave you,
and so you'll also watch me die.
Alas, for me! Yes, for me!
Sad cave so full of painful cries
wrung from me in my agony,
what will each day bring to me now?
Where will I find my nourishment   [1090]
or any hope of getting food?

πέλειαι δ᾽ ἄνω
πτωκάδες ὀξυτόνου διὰ πνεύματος
ἑλῶσιν· οὐκέτ᾽ ἴσχω.

ΧΟΡΟΣ

σύ τοι σύ τοι κατηξίωσας,   1095
ὦ βαρύποτμε, κοὐκ
ἄλλοθεν ἔχει τύχα τᾷδ᾽ ἀπὸ μείζονος,
εὖτέ γε παρὸν φρονῆσαι
τοῦ λῴονος δαίμονος εἵλου τὸ κάκιον αἰνεῖν.   1100

ΦΙΛΟΚΤΗΤΗΣ

ὦ τλάμων τλάμων ἄρ᾽ ἐγὼ
καὶ μόχθῳ λωβατός, ὃς ἤδη μετ᾽ οὐδενὸς ὕστερον
ἀνδρῶν εἰσοπίσω τάλας ναίων ἐνθάδ᾽ ὀλοῦμαι,
αἰαῖ αἰαῖ,   1106
οὐ φορβὰν ἔτι προσφέρων,
οὐ πτανῶν ἀπ᾽ ἐμῶν ὅπλων
κραταιαῖς μετὰ χερσὶν   1110
ἴσχων· ἀλλά μοι ἄσκοπα
κρυπτά τ᾽ ἔπη δολερᾶς ὑπέδυ φρενός·
ἰδοίμαν δέ νιν,
τὸν τάδε μησάμενον, τὸν ἴσον χρόνον
ἐμὰς λαχόντ᾽ ἀνίας.   1115

ΧΟΡΟΣ

πότμος, πότμος σε δαιμόνων τάδ᾽,
οὐδὲ σέ γε δόλος,
ἔσχεν ὑπὸ χειρὸς ἀμᾶς. στυγερὰν ἔχε
δύσποτμον ἀρὰν ἐπ᾽ ἄλλοις.   1120
καὶ γὰρ ἐμοὶ τοῦτο μέλει, μὴ φιλότητ᾽ ἀπώσῃ.

ΦΙΛΟΚΤΗΤΗΣ

οἴμοι μοι, καί που πολιᾶς
πόντου θινὸς ἐφήμενος
ἐγγελᾷ, χερὶ πάλλων   1125
τὰν ἐμὰν μελέου τροφάν,
τὰν οὐδείς ποτ᾽ ἐβάστασεν.
ὦ τόξον φίλον, ὦ φίλων

Wild pigeons will cross overhead
and fly on past through piercing winds—
I can no longer shoot them down.

CHORUS

You've brought this on yourself,
ill-fated man—your grievous luck
arises from no other source,
nor from a man with greater strength.
You could have been more sensible.
But no—you'd rather have a grimmer fate
when you might have chosen better.   [1100]

PHILOCTETES

Then I'm a miserable man,
truly miserable, beaten down
by hardships I've been through.
So from now on I'll live and die,
a suffering man, with no one else.
Alas, for all my pain!
I can no longer bring my food
to where I dwell, no longer
can I hold my feathered weapons
in my strong hands. A crafty mind
has tricked me with deceiving lies.
I wish that I might see the man
who planned this scheme condemned
to bear my pain for just as long!

CHORUS

This is your fate set by the gods.
You've not been tricked by hands of mine.
So aim your dreadful fatal curse   [1120]
at other men. What most concerns me
is if you now cease to be my friend.

PHILOCTETES

Alas for me! I see him now—
sitting beside the salt white ocean shore,
laughing at me, as he waves the bow
which fed me in my wretched life,
which no one else had ever held.
O my lovely bow, my friend,

χειρῶν ἐκβεβιασμένον,
ἦ που ἐλεινὸν ὁρᾷς, φρένας εἴ τινας   1130
ἔχεις, τὸν Ἡράκλειον
ἄρθμιον ὧδέ σοι
οὐκέτι χρησόμενον τὸ μεθύστερον,
ἄλλου δ᾽ ἐν μεταλλαγᾷ
πολυμηχάνου ἀνδρὸς ἐρέσσει,   1135
ὁρῶν μὲν αἰσχρὰς ἀπάτας, στυγνὸν δὲ φῶτ᾽
    ἐχθοδοπόν,
μυρί᾽, ἀπ᾽ αἰσχρῶν ἀνατέλλονθ᾽, ὃς ἐφ᾽ ἡμῖν κάκ᾽
    ἐμήσατ᾽, ὦ Ζεῦ.

ΧΟΡΟΣ

ἀνδρός τοι τὰ μὲν ἔνδικ᾽ αἰὲν εἰπεῖν,   1140
εἰπόντος δὲ μὴ φθονερὰν
ἐξῶσαι γλώσσας ὀδύναν.
κεῖνος δ᾽ εἷς ἀπὸ πολλῶν
ταχθεὶς τῶνδ᾽ ἐφημοσύνᾳ
κοινὰν ἤνυσεν ἐς φίλους ἀρωγάν.   1145

ΦΙΛΟΚΤΗΤΗΣ

ὦ πταναὶ θῆραι χαροπῶν τ᾽
ἔθνη θηρῶν, οὓς ὅδ᾽ ἔχει
χῶρος οὐρεσιβώτας,
μηκέτ᾽ ἀπ᾽ αὐλίων φυγᾷ
πηδᾶτ᾽· οὐ γὰρ ἔχω χεροῖν   1150
τὰν πρόσθεν βελέων ἀλκάν,
ὦ δύστανος ἐγὼ τανῦν,
ἀλλ᾽ ἀνέδην, ὁ δὲ χῶρος ἄρ᾽ οὐκέτι
φοβητὸς οὐκέθ᾽ ὑμῖν,
ἔρπετε· νῦν καλὸν   1155
ἀντίφονον κορέσαι στόμα πρὸς χάριν
ἐμᾶς σαρκὸς αἰόλας·
ἀπὸ γὰρ βίον αὐτίκα λείψω.
πόθεν γὰρ ἔσται βιοτά; τίς ὧδ᾽ ἐν αὔραις τρέφεται,   1160
μηκέτι μηδενὸς κρατύνων ὅσα πέμπει βιόδωρος αἶα;

wrenched from these loving hands,
if you had power to understand,   [1130]
you'd feel such pity as you looked on me,
for Hercules' friend no more
will from now on be using you.
Another man will handle you,
a man of much deceit. You'll see
his shameless tricks, his hateful face,
that enemy whom I despise,
whose plans have injured me so much,
the effects of his disgraceful skill.
O Zeus!

CHORUS
          A man should say what's right and useful,   [1140]
and, as he does, his tongue should never speak
malicious, hurtful slurs. Odysseus
was made the single representative
for many men, and, at their command,
has brought his friends a common benefit.

PHILOCTETES
You feathered birds, you flocks of bright-eyed beasts
who graze up on the hillside slopes,
no longer will you spring from me
and run away from your own dens.   [1150]
My hands no longer grip those shafts
which gave me power before,
and now my plight is desperate.
You're free to roam around at will,
with nothing more to make you fear.
And now you should take blood for blood,
yes, take your time and gorge yourself
on my contaminated flesh.
My life I'll give up soon enough.
Where can I find my nourishment?
For who can feed himself on winds,   [1160]
once he no longer has those things
which earth, who gives us life, provides?

ΧΟΡΟΣ

πρὸς θεῶν, εἴ τι σέβει ξένον, πέλασσον,
εὐνοίᾳ πάσᾳ πελάταν·
ἀλλὰ γνῶθ᾽, εὖ γνῶθ᾽ ἐπὶ σοὶ   1165
κῆρα τάνδ᾽ ἀποφεύγειν.
οἰκτρὰ γὰρ βόσκειν, ἀδαὴς δ᾽
ἔχειν μυρίον ἄχθος, ὃ ξυνοικεῖ.

ΦΙΛΟΚΤΗΤΗΣ

πάλιν πάλιν παλαιὸν ἄλγημ᾽ ὑπέμνασας, ὦ   1170
λῷστε τῶν πρὶν ἐντόπων.
τί μ᾽ ὤλεσας; τί μ᾽ εἴργασαι;

ΧΟΡΟΣ

τί τοῦτ᾽ ἔλεξας;

ΦΙΛΟΚΤΗΤΗΣ

                    εἰ σὺ τὰν ἐμοὶ
στυγερὰν Τρῳάδα γᾶν μ᾽ ἤλπισας ἄξειν.   1175

ΧΟΡΟΣ

τόδε γὰρ νοῶ κράτιστον.

ΦΙΛΟΚΤΗΤΗΣ

                    ἀπό νύν με λείπετ᾽ ἤδη.

ΧΟΡΟΣ

φίλα μοι, φίλα ταῦτα παρήγγειλας ἑκόντι τε πράσσειν.
ἴωμεν ἴωμεν
ναὸς ἵν᾽ ἡμῖν τέτακται.   1180

ΦΙΛΟΚΤΗΤΗΣ

μή, πρὸς ἀραίου Διός, ἔλθῃς, ἱκετεύω.

CHORUS

    If you feel you can respect
    a stranger who comes up to you
    with all good will, then, by the gods,
    approach the man more closely.
    But know this—and keep it well in mind—
    it's up to you to evade that fate.
    To nourish it with your own flesh
    is pitiful, and there's no way
    you can endure the countless pains
    that live within your body.

PHILOCTETES

    You remind me one more time again
    of that old agonizing thought,   [1170]
    though you are nicer than those men
    who visited this place before.
    Why have you destroyed my life?
    What have you done to me?

CHORUS

    What do you mean?

PHILOCTETES

    You hoped to take me off to Troy,
    a land which I despise.

CHORUS

                        Yes.
    I think that would be best.

PHILOCTETES

    Then go away. Leave me at once.

CHORUS

    Well, that's all right with me—in fact,
    I like the order you just gave.
    I'll do it willingly. Let's go.
    Let's be off—and every sailor move   [1180]
    to his own station onboard ship.

[The CHORUS turns and starts moving off]

PHILOCTETES

    No, don't go. I'm begging you,
    in the name of Zeus, the god
    who hears men's curses.

ΧΟΡΟΣ

μετρίαζ᾽.

ΦΙΛΟΚΤΗΤΗΣ

ὦ ξένοι, μείνατε, πρὸς θεῶν.

ΧΟΡΟΣ

τί θροεῖς;   1185

ΦΙΛΟΚΤΗΤΗΣ

αἰαῖ αἰαῖ,
δαίμων δαίμων· ἀπόλωλ᾽ ὁ τάλας·
ὦ πούς πούς, τί σ᾽ ἔτ᾽ ἐν βίῳ
τεύξω τῷ μετόπιν τάλας;
ὦ ξένοι, ἔλθετ᾽ ἐπήλυδες αὖθις.   1190

ΧΟΡΟΣ

τί ῥέξοντες ἀλλοκότῳ
γνώμᾳ τῶν πάρος, ὧν προύφαινες;

ΦΙΛΟΚΤΗΤΗΣ

οὔτοι νεμεσητόν,
ἀλύοντα χειμερίῳ
λύπᾳ καὶ παρὰ νοῦν θροεῖν.   1195

ΧΟΡΟΣ

βᾶθί νυν, ὦ τάλαν, ὥς σε κελεύομεν.

ΦΙΛΟΚΤΗΤΗΣ

οὐδέποτ᾽ οὐδέποτ᾽, ἴσθι τόδ᾽ ἔμπεδον,
οὐδ᾽ εἰ πυρφόρος ἀστεροπητὴς
βροντᾶς αὐγαῖς μ᾽ εἶσι φλογίζων.
ἐρρέτω Ἴλιον οἵ θ᾽ ὑπ᾽ ἐκείνῳ   1200
πάντες ὅσοι τόδ᾽ ἔτλασαν ἐμοῦ ποδὸς ἄρθρον ἀπῶσαι.
ἀλλ᾽, ὦ ξένοι, ἕν γέ μοι εὖχος ὀρέξατε.

ΧΟΡΟΣ

ποῖον ἐρεῖς τόδ᾽ ἔπος;

CHORUS

              Calm down.

PHILOCTETES

    O strangers, by the gods, stay here.

CHORUS

    Why are you calling?

PHILOCTETES

              Aaaaiiii . . . aaaaiiii . . .
    That demon's killing me . . . savage god . . .
    my foot . . . this foot of mine . . .
    how shall I deal with you
    in what remains to me of life?
    O friends, return to me again.   [1190]
    Come back!

CHORUS

           What should we do?
    Do you have something else in mind
    that alters what you said before?

PHILOCTETES

    You should not grow indignant
    when someone in a storm of pain
    says things that make no sense.

CHORUS

    Then, you unhappy man, come with us,
    as we are asking you.

PHILOCTETES

           Never! Never!
    That you can be sure of! No, not even
    if the lord of blazing lightning comes
    ready to blast me with his fiery thunder.
    Damn Troy and all those warriors there,   [1200]
    before the city, who dared throw away
    this poor lame foot of mine. But, friends,
    please grant me one request I have.

CHORUS

    What request is that?

ΦΙΛΟΚΤΗΤΗΣ
           ξίφος, εἴ ποθεν,
ἢ γένυν ἢ βελέων τι προπέμψατε.   1205

ΧΟΡΟΣ
  ὡς τίνα δὴ ῥέξῃς παλάμαν ποτέ;

ΦΙΛΟΚΤΗΤΗΣ
  χρῶτ' ἀπὸ πάντα καὶ ἄρθρα τέμω χερί·
  φονᾷ φονᾷ νόος ἤδη.

ΧΟΡΟΣ
  τί ποτε;

ΦΙΛΟΚΤΗΤΗΣ
      πατέρα ματεύων.

ΧΟΡΟΣ
  ποῖ γᾶς;   1210

ΦΙΛΟΚΤΗΤΗΣ
     ἐς Ἅιδου·
  οὐ γάρ ἐστ' ἐν φάει γ' ἔτι.
  ὦ πόλις, ὦ πατρία,
  πῶς ἂν εἰσίδοιμ' ἄθλιός σ' ἀνήρ,
  ὅς γε σὰν λιπὼν ἱερὰν   1215
  λιβάδ' ἐχθροῖς ἔβαν Δαναοῖς
  ἀρωγός· ἔτ' οὐδέν εἰμι.

ΧΟΡΟΣ
  ἐγὼ μὲν ἤδη καὶ πάλαι νεὼς ὁμοῦ
  στείχων ἂν ἦ σοι τῆς ἐμῆς, εἰ μὴ πέλας
  Ὀδυσσέα στείχοντα τόν τ' Ἀχιλλέως
  γόνον πρὸς ἡμᾶς δεῦρ' ἰόντ' ἐλεύσσομεν.   1220

PHILOCTETES

              Give me a sword,
if you have one there, or else an axe—
any weapon will do.

CHORUS

             What is your plan?
Some drastic act?

PHILOCTETES

                Hack at my flesh
and cut these bones apart, all of them.
To die, yes, my mind now thinks on death.

CHORUS

But why do that?   [1210]

PHILOCTETES

          To find my father.

CHORUS

Where does he live?

PHILOCTETES

             He is in Hades.
He cannot still be living in the light.
O my city, city of my fathers,
how I wish that I could see you now—
I brought myself such misery
the day I left your sacred river,
to help Danaans, my enemies.
I'm nothing anymore, nothing.

[PHILOCTETES exits into his cave, leaving the CHORUS alone on stage]

CHORUS

I'd have left you here some time ago
and gone back to my ship, if I'd not seen
Odysseus coming and bringing with him   [1220]
Achilles' son. They're getting close to us.

[Enter NEOPTOLEMUS and ODYSSEUS. NEOPTOLEMUS is still carrying Philoctetes' bow and arrows]

Sophocles

ΟΔΥΣΣΕΥΣ
  οὐκ ἂν φράσειας ἥντιν' αὖ παλίντροπος
  κέλευθον ἕρπεις ὧδε σὺν σπουδῇ ταχύς;

ΝΕΟΠΤΟΛΕΜΟΣ
  λύσων ὅσ' ἐξήμαρτον ἐν τῷ πρὶν χρόνῳ.

ΟΔΥΣΣΕΥΣ
  δεινόν γε φωνεῖς· ἡ δ' ἁμαρτία τίς ἦν;

ΝΕΟΠΤΟΛΕΜΟΣ
  ἣν σοὶ πιθόμενος τῷ τε σύμπαντι στρατῷ   1225

ΟΔΥΣΣΕΥΣ
  ἔπραξας ἔργον ποῖον ὧν οὔ σοι πρέπον;

ΝΕΟΠΤΟΛΕΜΟΣ
  ἀπάταισιν αἰσχραῖς ἄνδρα καὶ δόλοις ἑλών.

ΟΔΥΣΣΕΥΣ
  τὸν ποῖον; ὤμοι· μῶν τι βουλεύει νέον;

ΝΕΟΠΤΟΛΕΜΟΣ
  νέον μὲν οὐδέν, τῷ δὲ Ποίαντος τόκῳ,   1230

ΟΔΥΣΣΕΥΣ
  τί χρῆμα δράσεις; ὥς μ' ὑπῆλθέ τις φόβος.

ΝΕΟΠΤΟΛΕΜΟΣ
  παρ' οὗπερ ἔλαβον τάδε τὰ τόξ', αὖθις πάλιν

ΟΔΥΣΣΕΥΣ
  ὦ Ζεῦ, τί λέξεις; οὔ τί που δοῦναι νοεῖς;

ΝΕΟΠΤΟΛΕΜΟΣ
  αἰσχρῶς γὰρ αὐτὰ κοὐ δίκῃ λαβὼν ἔχω.

ΟΔΥΣΣΕΥΣ
  πρὸς θεῶν, πότερα δὴ κερτομῶν λέγεις τάδε;   1235

ODYSSEUS

    Why are you coming back along this path
    at such a rapid pace?

NEOPTOLEMUS

                    I was wrong before.
    I have to fix all those mistakes I made.

ODYSSEUS

    You sound odd. What mistakes are those?

NEOPTOLEMUS

    When I obeyed you and the entire army.

ODYSSEUS

    What error did you make that shamed you so?

NEOPTOLEMUS

    I used disgraceful lies and sly deceit
    to catch a man.

ODYSSEUS

               What sort of man? Oh, oh.
    Are you devising some foolhardy scheme?

NEOPTOLEMUS

    No, nothing rash. But with Poeas' son . . .   [1230]

ODYSSEUS *[interrupting]*

    What are you going to do? A certain fear
    has just occurred to me . . .

NEOPTOLEMUS

             . . . whose bow I took . . .
    return it.

ODYSSEUS

           By Zeus, what are you saying?
    You don't intend to hand it back to him?

NEOPTOLEMUS

    Yes. I got it in a shameful manner,
    and it's not right for me to keep it.

ODYSSEUS

    By the gods, are you saying this to mock me?

ΝΕΟΠΤΟΛΕΜΟΣ

εἰ κερτόμησίς ἐστι τἀληθῆ λέγειν.

ΟΔΥΣΣΕΥΣ

τί φῄς, Ἀχιλλέως παῖ; τίν' εἴρηκας λόγον;

ΝΕΟΠΤΟΛΕΜΟΣ

δὶς ταὐτὰ βούλει καὶ τρὶς ἀναπολεῖν μ' ἔπη;

ΟΔΥΣΣΕΥΣ

ἀρχὴν κλύειν ἂν οὐδ' ἅπαξ ἐβουλόμην.

ΝΕΟΠΤΟΛΕΜΟΣ

εὖ νῦν ἐπίστω πάντ' ἀκηκοὼς λόγον.   1240

ΟΔΥΣΣΕΥΣ

ἔστιν τις, ἔστιν ὅς σε κωλύσει τὸ δρᾶν.

ΝΕΟΠΤΟΛΕΜΟΣ

τί φῄς; τίς ἔσται μ' οὑπικωλύσων τάδε;

ΟΔΥΣΣΕΥΣ

ξύμπας Ἀχαιῶν λαός, ἐν δὲ τοῖς ἐγώ.

ΝΕΟΠΤΟΛΕΜΟΣ

σοφὸς πεφυκὼς οὐδὲν ἐξαυδᾷς σοφόν.

ΟΔΥΣΣΕΥΣ

σὺ δ' οὔτε φωνεῖς οὔτε δρασείεις σοφά.   1245

ΝΕΟΠΤΟΛΕΜΟΣ

ἀλλ' εἰ δίκαια, τῶν σοφῶν κρείσσω τάδε.

ΟΔΥΣΣΕΥΣ

καὶ πῶς δίκαιον, ἅ γ' ἔλαβες βουλαῖς ἐμαῖς,
πάλιν μεθεῖναι ταῦτα;

NEOPTOLEMUS
Only if it's mockery to speak the truth.

ODYSSEUS
Son of Achilles, what are you saying?
What do you mean?

NEOPTOLEMUS
                              Do I really need
to say the same thing two or three times over?

ODYSSEUS
I did not want to hear it even once.

NEOPTOLEMUS
Well, you must clearly understand it now—   [1240]
for you've heard all I have to say.

ODYSSEUS
                              There are those
who will prevent you carrying that out.

NEOPTOLEMUS
What are you saying? Who will try to stop me?

ODYSSEUS
The whole Achaean army—including me.

NEOPTOLEMUS
You were born wise, but there's no wisdom now
in what you say.

ODYSSEUS
                              But these words of yours
and what you plan to do are most imprudent.

NEOPTOLEMUS
But if they're right, then they're more powerful
than wisdom.

ODYSSEUS
                              How can it be right and just,
to give back what you won thanks to my plan?

Sophocles

ΝΕΟΠΤΟΛΕΜΟΣ

τὴν ἁμαρτίαν

αἰσχρὰν ἁμαρτὼν ἀναλαβεῖν πειράσομαι.

ΟΔΥΣΣΕΥΣ

στρατὸν δ᾽ Ἀχαιῶν οὐ φοβεῖ, πράσσων τάδε;   1250

ΝΕΟΠΤΟΛΕΜΟΣ

ξὺν τῷ δικαίῳ τὸν σὸν οὐ ταρβῶ φόβον.

ΟΔΥΣΣΕΥΣ

[ξὺν τῷ δικαίῳ χεὶρ ἐμή σ᾽ ἀναγκάσει.]

ΝΕΟΠΤΟΛΕΜΟΣ

ἀλλ᾽ οὐδέ τοι σῇ χειρὶ πείθομαι τὸ δρᾶν.

ΟΔΥΣΣΕΥΣ

οὔ τἄρα Τρωσίν, ἀλλὰ σοὶ μαχούμεθα.

ΝΕΟΠΤΟΛΕΜΟΣ

ἴτω τὸ μέλλον.   1255

ΟΔΥΣΣΕΥΣ

χεῖρα δεξιὰν ὁρᾷς

κώπης ἐπιψαύουσαν;

ΝΕΟΠΤΟΛΕΜΟΣ

ἀλλὰ κἀμέ τοι

ταὐτὸν τόδ᾽ ὄψει δρῶντα κοὐ μέλλοντ᾽ ἔτι.

ΟΔΥΣΣΕΥΣ

καίτοι σ᾽ ἐάσω· τῷ δὲ σύμπαντι στρατῷ

λέξω τάδ᾽ ἐλθών, ὅς σε τιμωρήσεται.

ΝΕΟΠΤΟΛΕΜΟΣ

ἐσωφρόνησας· κἂν τὰ λοίφ᾽ οὕτω φρονῇς,   1260

ἴσως ἂν ἐκτὸς κλαυμάτων ἔχοις πόδα.

σὺ δ᾽, ὦ Ποίαντος παῖ, Φιλοκτήτην λέγω,

ἔξελθ᾽, ἀμείψας τάσδε πετρήρεις στέγας.

110

NEOPTOLEMUS

    I made a mistake and lost my honour—
    I must try to get it back.

ODYSSEUS

                        If you do try,   [1250]
    aren't you afraid of the Achaean troops?

NEOPTOLEMUS

    With justice at my side, I do not fear
    the danger you describe.

ODYSSEUS

                     [Your justice!
    My hand will make that justice bend to me.][23]

NEOPTOLEMUS

    Even so, I won't obey those arms of yours.
    I won't do what you ask.

ODYSSEUS

               Well, then, our fight
    is not against the Trojans but with you.

NEOPTOLEMUS

    If that's what it has to be, so be it.

ODYSSEUS

    Do you see my right hand resting on my sword?

NEOPTOLEMUS

    You'll see me doing the same. I won't hesitate.

ODYSSEUS

    All right, for now I'll leave you. But I'll go
    and tell the army what is happening here.
    And they will punish you.

NEOPTOLEMUS

                Now you're reasonable.
    If you keep up this frame of mind in future,
    perhaps you will not wander into trouble.   [1260]

[Odysseus moves away, as if leaving for the ship, but conceals himself and observes what now happens]

ΦΙΛΟΚΤΗΤΗΣ

τίς αὖ παρ᾽ ἄντροις θόρυβος ἵσταται βοῆς;

τί μ᾽ ἐκκαλεῖσθε; τοῦ κεχρημένοι, ξένοι;   1265

ὤμοι· κακὸν τὸ χρῆμα. μῶν τί μοι νέα

πάρεστε πρὸς κακοῖσι πέμποντες κακά;

ΝΕΟΠΤΟΛΕΜΟΣ

θάρσει· λόγους δ᾽ ἄκουσον οὓς ἥκω φέρων.

ΦΙΛΟΚΤΗΤΗΣ

δέδοικ᾽ ἔγωγε· καὶ τὰ πρὶν γὰρ ἐκ λόγων

καλῶν κακῶς ἔπραξα, σοῖς πεισθεὶς λόγοις.   1270

ΝΕΟΠΤΟΛΕΜΟΣ

οὔκουν ἔνεστι καὶ μεταγνῶναι πάλιν;

ΦΙΛΟΚΤΗΤΗΣ

τοιοῦτος ἦσθα τοῖς λόγοισι χὤτε μου

τὰ τόξ᾽ ἔκλεπτες, πιστός, ἀτηρὸς λάθρᾳ.

ΝΕΟΠΤΟΛΕΜΟΣ

ἀλλ᾽ οὔ τι μὴν νῦν· βούλομαι δέ σου κλύειν,

πότερα δέδοκταί σοι μένοντι καρτερεῖν   1275

ἢ πλεῖν μεθ᾽ ἡμῶν;

ΦΙΛΟΚΤΗΤΗΣ

                παῦε, μὴ λέξῃς πέρα·

μάτην γὰρ ἂν εἴπῃς γε πάντ᾽ εἰρήσεται.

ΝΕΟΠΤΟΛΕΜΟΣ

οὕτω δέδοκται;

NEOPTOLEMUS *[calling up to the cave]*
>You there, son of Poeas . . . I'm calling you.
>Philoctetes . . . Come out. Leave that rock
>you call your home.

PHILOCTETES *[from inside the cave]*
>   Now who's standing there
>making an unruly noise outside the cave?
>Why are you calling me? What do you want?

[PHILOCTETES partly emerges from the cave and sees Neoptolemus]

>O no! This is a wretched business.
>Are you here to bring me some new trouble
>on top of all the others?

NEOPTOLEMUS
>   Don't despair.
>Listen to the news I bring.

PHILOCTETES
>   I'm afraid.
>Fine words brought me disaster once before,
>when I trusted what you said.

NEOPTOLEMUS
>   But now
>is there no way I can apologize?   [1270]

PHILOCTETES
>You used words like that and stole my bow.
>You won my confidence, but secretly
>you worked for my destruction.

NEOPTOLEMUS
>But now I'm not like that. I wish to learn
>whether you want to stay on living here,
>enduring these conditions, or sail with us.

PHILOCTETES
>Stop there. Do not speak any more. Your words
>will all be wasted.

NEOPTOLEMUS
>   You are quite sure of that.

ΦΙΛΟΚΤΗΤΗΣ

    καὶ πέρα γ᾽ ἴσθ᾽ ἢ λέγω.

ΝΕΟΠΤΟΛΕΜΟΣ

    ἀλλ᾽ ἤθελον μὲν ἄν σε πεισθῆναι λόγοις
    ἐμοῖσιν· εἰ δὲ μή τι πρὸς καιρὸν λέγων
    κυρῶ, πέπαυμαι.

ΦΙΛΟΚΤΗΤΗΣ

            πάντα γὰρ φράσεις μάτην.   1280
    οὐ γάρ ποτ᾽ εὔνουν τὴν ἐμὴν κτήσει φρένα,
    ὅστις γ᾽ ἐμοῦ δόλοισι τὸν βίον λαβὼν
    ἀπεστέρηκας, κᾆτα νουθετεῖς ἐμὲ
    ἐλθών, ἀρίστου πατρὸς αἴσχιστος γεγώς.
    ὄλοισθ᾽, Ἀτρεῖδαι μὲν μάλιστ᾽, ἔπειτα δὲ   1285
    ὁ Λαρτίου παῖς καὶ σύ.

ΝΕΟΠΤΟΛΕΜΟΣ

               μὴ ᾽πεύξῃ πέρα·
    δέχου δὲ χειρὸς ἐξ ἐμῆς βέλη τάδε.

ΦΙΛΟΚΤΗΤΗΣ

    πῶς εἶπας; ἆρα δεύτερον δολούμεθα;

ΝΕΟΠΤΟΛΕΜΟΣ

    ἀπώμοσ᾽ ἁγνὸν Ζηνὸς ὑψίστου σέβας.

ΦΙΛΟΚΤΗΤΗΣ

    ὦ φίλτατ᾽ εἰπών, εἰ λέγεις ἐτήτυμα.   1290

ΝΕΟΠΤΟΛΕΜΟΣ

    τοὔργον παρέσται φανερόν· ἀλλὰ δεξιὰν
    πρότεινε χεῖρα, καὶ κράτει τῶν σῶν ὅπλων.

ΟΔΥΣΣΕΥΣ

    ἐγὼ δ᾽ ἀπαυδῶ γ᾽, ὦ θεοὶ ξυνίστορες,
    ὑπέρ τ᾽ Ἀτρειδῶν τοῦ τε σύμπαντος στρατοῦ.

PHILOCTETES

    Yes, I am—more sure than any words can say.

NEOPTOLEMUS

    I wish my words could have persuaded you.
    But if there's nothing I can say to help,
    then I will stop.

PHILOCTETES

                Everything you say is useless.   [1280]
    You'll never win my confidence, not now
    you've taken away my livelihood, robbed me
    and with a trick. Then you come over here
    to give me your advice, you shameless son
    of such a noble father. May you all die—
    the sons of Atreus first, then Laertes' son,
    then you.

NEOPTOLEMUS

            Stop making all those curses,
    and take these weapons from my hand.

PHILOCTETES

    What do you mean? Am I being tricked again?

NEOPTOLEMUS

    No. I swear by the sacred majesty of Zeus.

PHILOCTETES

    Such welcome words, if what you say is true.   [1290]

NEOPTOLEMUS

    My actions will show that. Put out your hand
    and take your weapons back.

[As Neoptolemus hands the bow to Philoctetes, Odysseus re-emerges from his hiding place and moves forward]

ODYSSEUS

              No!
    In the name of the sons of Atreus
    and the whole army, I'm telling you no,
    as gods are witnesses for me!

Sophocles

ΦΙΛΟΚΤΗΤΗΣ

τέκνον, τίνος φώνημα, μῶν Ὀδυσσέως,　　　　1295
ἐπῃσθόμην;

ΟΔΥΣΣΕΥΣ

　　　　σάφ᾽ ἴσθι· καὶ πέλας γ᾽ ὁρᾷς,
ὅς σ᾽ ἐς τὰ Τροίας πεδί᾽ ἀποστελῶ βίᾳ,
ἐάν τ᾽ Ἀχιλλέως παῖς ἐάν τε μὴ θέλῃ·

ΦΙΛΟΚΤΗΤΗΣ

ἀλλ᾽ οὔ τι χαίρων, ἢν τόδ᾽ ὀρθωθῇ βέλος.　　　　1300

ΝΕΟΠΤΟΛΕΜΟΣ

ἆ, μηδαμῶς, μή, πρὸς θεῶν, μεθῇς βέλος.

ΦΙΛΟΚΤΗΤΗΣ

μέθες με, πρὸς θεῶν, χεῖρα, φίλτατον τέκνον.

ΝΕΟΠΤΟΛΕΜΟΣ

οὐκ ἂν μεθείην.

ΦΙΛΟΚΤΗΤΗΣ

　　　　φεῦ· τί μ᾽ ἄνδρα πολέμιον
ἐχθρόν τ᾽ ἀφείλου μὴ κτανεῖν τόξοις ἐμοῖς;

ΝΕΟΠΤΟΛΕΜΟΣ

ἀλλ᾽ οὔτ᾽ ἐμοὶ τοῦτ᾽ ἐστὶν οὔτε σοὶ καλόν.　　　　1305

ΦΙΛΟΚΤΗΤΗΣ

ἀλλ᾽ οὖν τοσοῦτόν γ᾽ ἴσθι, τοὺς πρώτους στρατοῦ,
τοὺς τῶν Ἀχαιῶν ψευδοκήρυκας, κακοὺς
ὄντας πρὸς αἰχμήν, ἐν δὲ τοῖς λόγοις θρασεῖς.

ΝΕΟΠΤΟΛΕΜΟΣ

εἶεν· τὰ μὲν δὴ τόξ᾽ ἔχεις, κοὐκ ἔσθ᾽ ὅτου
ὀργὴν ἔχοις ἂν οὐδὲ μέμψιν εἰς ἐμέ.

PHILOCTETES

My lad,
who was that speaking? Was it Odysseus?

ODYSSEUS *[moving forward]*
Yes. It is me. Now you can see up close
the man who'll take you off to Troy by force,
whether Achilles' son wants that or not.

PHILOCTETES *[putting an arrow to his bow string]*
That won't bring you any joy, if this arrow
flies straight, directly to its mark.

*[ODYSSEUS moves away to hide again. NEOPTOLEMUS grabs
PHILOCTETES to stop him shooting his arrow]*

NEOPTOLEMUS
By the gods, don't shoot that arrow off.   [1300]

PHILOCTETES
In the name of the gods, dear lad, let go.

NEOPTOLEMUS *[continuing to restrain Philoctetes]*
No, I won't.

PHILOCTETES
Alas! Why did you spoil
my chance to use this bow of mine to kill
that enemy I hate?

NEOPTOLEMUS
That would mean disaster
for both of us, for you and me.

PHILOCTETES
You should know
the army's leaders, lying spokesmen for the Greeks,
though bold in speech, are cowards in a fight.

NEOPTOLEMUS
That may be true. But now you have the bow,
you have no reason to be angry with me
or complain about my conduct.

Sophocles

ΦΙΛΟΚΤΗΤΗΣ

ξύμφημι· τὴν φύσιν δ᾽ ἔδειξας, ὦ τέκνον,   1310
ἐξ ἧς ἔβλαστες, οὐχὶ Σισύφου πατρός,
ἀλλ᾽ ἐξ Ἀχιλλέως, ὃς μετὰ ζώντων ὅτ᾽ ἦν
ἤκου᾽ ἄριστα, νῦν δὲ τῶν τεθνηκότων.

ΝΕΟΠΤΟΛΕΜΟΣ

ἥσθην πατέρα τὸν ἀμὸν εὐλογοῦντά σε
αὐτόν τ᾽ ἔμ᾽· ὧν δέ σου τυχεῖν ἐφίεμαι,   1315
ἄκουσον. ἀνθρώποισι τὰς μὲν ἐκ θεῶν
τύχας δοθείσας ἔστ᾽ ἀναγκαῖον φέρειν·
ὅσοι δ᾽ ἑκουσίοισιν ἔγκεινται βλάβαις,
ὥσπερ σύ, τούτοις οὔτε συγγνώμην ἔχειν
δίκαιόν ἐστιν οὔτ᾽ ἐποικτίρειν τινά.   1320
σὺ δ᾽ ἠγρίωσαι, κοὔτε σύμβουλον δέχει,
ἐάν τε νουθετῇ τις εὐνοίᾳ λέγων,
στυγεῖς, πολέμιον δυσμενῆ θ᾽ ἡγούμενος.
ὅμως δὲ λέξω· Ζῆνα δ᾽ ὅρκιον καλῶ·
καὶ ταῦτ᾽ ἐπίστω καὶ γράφου φρενῶν ἔσω.   1325
σὺ γὰρ νοσεῖς τόδ᾽ ἄλγος ἐκ θείας τύχης,
Χρύσης πελασθεὶς φύλακος, ὃς τὸν ἀκαλυφῆ
σηκὸν φυλάσσει κρύφιος οἰκουρῶν ὄφις·
καὶ παῦλαν ἴσθι τῆσδε μή ποτ᾽ ἂν τυχεῖν
νόσου βαρείας, ἕως ἂν αὐτὸς ἥλιος   1330
ταύτῃ μὲν αἴρῃ, τῇδε δ᾽ αὖ δύνῃ πάλιν,
πρὶν ἂν τὰ Τροίας πεδί᾽ ἑκὼν αὐτὸς μόλῃς,
καὶ τοῖν παρ᾽ ἡμῖν ἐντυχὼν Ἀσκληπίδαιν
νόσου μαλαχθῇς τῆσδε, καὶ τὰ πέργαμα
ξὺν τοῖσδε τόξοις ξύν τ᾽ ἐμοὶ πέρσας φανῇς.   1335
ὡς δ᾽ οἶδα ταῦτα τῇδ᾽ ἔχοντ᾽ ἐγὼ φράσω.
ἀνὴρ γὰρ ἡμῖν ἐστιν ἐκ Τροίας ἁλούς,
Ἕλενος ἀριστόμαντις, ὃς λέγει σαφῶς
ὡς δεῖ γενέσθαι ταῦτα· καὶ πρὸς τοῖσδ᾽ ἔτι

PHILOCTETES

                          I agree.   [1310]
My lad, you've shown the family lineage
you sprang from. Your father was not Sisyphus.
No, you come from Achilles, who, in his life,
had the finest reputation of them all,
just as he now has among the dead.

NEOPTOLEMUS

    I'm pleased to hear you praise my father
and me, as well. But pay attention now
to what I'd like from you. Men must endure
those fortunes given to them by the gods.
But when they insist on injuring themselves,
the way you're doing now, then it's not right
to pity or excuse them. You've become   [1320]
a savage man, rejecting all advice.
If someone who's a friend of yours speaks up
and says you're doing wrong, you hate the man.
You call him your enemy, a traitor.
But still, I'll speak to you, invoking Zeus,
who punishes the men who break their oaths.
Keep these words in mind. Write them on your heart.
You've been suffering from this affliction
as fate sent from the gods, because you went
too close to Chryse's secret sentinel,
the snake which keeps watch where she lives and guards
her sacred precinct open to the sky.
Know this, too—you will never find an end
to this distressful agony of yours,
not while the sun still rises in the east   [1330]
and then sets in the west, until you come,
of your own free will, to the Trojan plain,
and there, among us, meet Asclepius' sons,
find relief from this disease, and with help
from me and from that bow be known to all
as the man who smashed the towers of Troy.[24]
I'll tell you how I come to know these things.
We took a Trojan man called Helenus,
an excellent prophet, who clearly states
these things must happen and, in addition,

119

Sophocles

ὡς ἔστ' ἀνάγκη τοῦ παρεστῶτος θέρους   1340
Τροίαν ἁλῶναι πᾶσαν· ἢ δίδωσ' ἑκὼν
κτείνειν ἑαυτόν, ἢν τάδε ψευσθῇ λέγων.
ταῦτ' οὖν ἐπεὶ κάτοισθα, συγχώρει θέλων.
καλὴ γὰρ ἡ 'πίκτησις, Ἑλλήνων ἕνα
κριθέντ' ἄριστον τοῦτο μὲν παιωνίας   1345
ἐς χεῖρας ἐλθεῖν, εἶτα τὴν πολύστονον
Τροίαν ἑλόντα κλέος ὑπέρτατον λαβεῖν.

ΦΙΛΟΚΤΗΤΗΣ

ὦ στυγνὸς αἰών, τί με, τί δῆτ' ἔχεις ἄνω
βλέποντα κοὐκ ἀφῆκας εἰς Ἅιδου μολεῖν;
οἴμοι, τί δράσω; πῶς ἀπιστήσω λόγοις   1350
τοῖς τοῦδ', ὃς εὔνους ὢν ἐμοὶ παρῄνεσεν;
ἀλλ' εἰκάθω δῆτ'; εἶτα πῶς ὁ δύσμορος
εἰς φῶς τάδ' ἔρξας εἶμι; τῷ προσήγορος;
πῶς, ὦ τὰ πάντ' ἰδόντες ἀμφ' ἐμοὶ κύκλοι,
ταῦτ' ἐξανασχήσεσθε, τοῖσιν Ἀτρέως   1355
ἐμὲ ξυνόντα παισίν, οἵ μ' ἀπώλεσαν;
πῶς τῷ πανώλει παιδὶ τῷ Λαερτίου;
οὐ γάρ με τἄλγος τῶν παρελθόντων δάκνει,
ἀλλ' οἷα χρὴ παθεῖν με πρὸς τούτων ἔτι
δοκῶ προλεύσσειν· οἷς γὰρ ἡ γνώμη κακῶν
μήτηρ γένηται, τἄλλα παιδεύει κακούς.   1360
καὶ σοῦ δ' ἔγωγε θαυμάσας ἔχω τόδε.
χρῆν γάρ σε μήτ' αὐτόν ποτ' ἐς Τροίαν μολεῖν
ἡμᾶς τ' ἀπείργειν, οἵ γέ σου καθύβρισαν,
πατρὸς γέρας συλῶντες, εἶτα τοῖσδε σὺ
εἶ ξυμμαχήσων, κἄμ' ἀναγκάζεις τόδε;   1365

120

predicts we will seize Troy this coming summer.
If his words prove false, he'll offer himself,
quite willingly, for slaughter. And so now
you understand these things, you should be willing
to concede. It's one more splendid honour.
You'll be judged the most exceptional man
among the Greeks—first, for coming there
to hands which healed you, then, more than that,
for capturing Troy, the source of so much grief.
You'll win the very highest fame there is.

PHILOCTETES

O hateful life, why keep me here above,
gazing at the light? Why not release me,
send me down to Hades? What shall I do?   [1350]
Alas! How can I distrust what this man says?
He's giving me advice as a good friend.
So, then, do I relent? If I do yield,
how can I, given my unhappy fate,
appear in public view? Who do I talk to?
You eyes of mine, who've witnessed everything
I've had to go through, how could you bear it,
to see me socializing with those men,
the sons of Atreus, who ruined me?
Or with Laertes' all-destroying son?

[Philoctetes addresses Neoptolemus directly]

It's not the pain of what I have endured
that gnaws at me—I seem to see ahead
all the things I'll have to suffer from them
from now on. Once a man's mind has become   [1360]
the mother of evil acts, it trains him
to deceive in everything that follows.
And in this matter I'm surprised at you.
You must never return to Troy yourself
and should prevent me going there. Those men
did you an injury by taking away
your father's weapons, when, in that contest
for his arms, they judged heart-broken Ajax
inferior to Odysseus. After that,
will you fight as their ally and force me

Sophocles

μὴ δῆτα, τέκνον· ἀλλ' ἅ μοι ξυνώμοσας,
πέμψον πρὸς οἴκους· καὐτὸς ἐν Σκύρῳ μένων
ἔα κακῶς αὐτοὺς ἀπόλλυσθαι κακούς.
χοὔτω διπλῆν μὲν ἐξ ἐμοῦ κτήσει χάριν,   1370
διπλῆν δὲ πατρός, κοὐ κακοὺς ἐπωφελῶν
δόξεις ὅμοιος τοῖς κακοῖς πεφυκέναι.

ΝΕΟΠΤΟΛΕΜΟΣ

λέγεις μὲν εἰκότ', ἀλλ' ὅμως σε βούλομαι
θεοῖς τε πιστεύσαντα τοῖς τ' ἐμοῖς λόγοις
φίλου μετ' ἀνδρὸς τοῦδε τῆσδ' ἐκπλεῖν χθονός.   1375

ΦΙΛΟΚΤΗΤΗΣ

ἦ πρὸς τὰ Τροίας πεδία καὶ τὸν Ἀτρέως
ἔχθιστον υἱὸν τῷδε δυστήνῳ ποδί;

ΝΕΟΠΤΟΛΕΜΟΣ

πρὸς τοὺς μὲν οὖν σε τήνδε τ' ἔμπυον βάσιν
παύσοντας ἄλγους κἀποσώσοντας νόσου.

ΦΙΛΟΚΤΗΤΗΣ

ὦ δεινὸν αἶνον αἰνέσας, τί φῂς ποτε;   1380

ΝΕΟΠΤΟΛΕΜΟΣ

ἃ σοί τε κἀμοὶ λῷσθ' ὁρῶ τελούμενα.

ΦΙΛΟΚΤΗΤΗΣ

καὶ ταῦτα λέξας οὐ καταισχύνει θεούς;

ΝΕΟΠΤΟΛΕΜΟΣ

πῶς γάρ τις αἰσχύνοιτ' ἂν ὠφελῶν φίλους·

ΦΙΛΟΚΤΗΤΗΣ

λέγεις δ' Ἀτρείδαις ὄφελος ἢ 'π' ἐμοὶ τόδε;

122

to do so, too? Do not do it, my son,
but take me home, as you have sworn to do.
Then you should keep yourself on Scyros
and leave those evil men to be destroyed
in their own cruel way. If you do that,   [1370]
you'll get double gratitude from me
and from my father, too. And you won't seem
because of how you helped those wicked men
to have an inbred nature just like theirs.

NEOPTOLEMUS
What you say makes good sense. But nonetheless,
I'd like you to rely upon the gods
and my own words and sail away from here
with me, your friend.

PHILOCTETES
                              You mean I should set off
with this disgusting foot to the Trojan plain
and that abominable son of Atreus?

NEOPTOLEMUS
No. You should go to those who'll end the pain
in that pus-filled foot of yours. They'll save you
from your sickness.

PHILOCTETES
                              The advice you're giving   [1380]
is frightening me. What are you saying?

NEOPTOLEMUS
I recognize what's best for you and me.

PHILOCTETES
When you say that, you don't feel any shame
before the gods?

NEOPTOLEMUS
                              How can a man feel shame
when he's helping out a friend of his?

PHILOCTETES
Are you talking about some benefit
for me or for the sons of Atreus?

Sophocles

ΝΕΟΠΤΟΛΕΜΟΣ
σοί που, φίλος γ' ὤν, χὠ λόγος τοιόσδε μου. 1385

ΦΙΛΟΚΤΗΤΗΣ
πῶς, ὅς γε τοῖς ἐχθροῖσί μ' ἐκδοῦναι θέλεις;

ΝΕΟΠΤΟΛΕΜΟΣ
ὦ τᾶν, διδάσκου μὴ θρασύνεσθαι κακοῖς.

ΦΙΛΟΚΤΗΤΗΣ
ὀλεῖς με, γιγνώσκω σε, τοῖσδε τοῖς λόγοις.

ΝΕΟΠΤΟΛΕΜΟΣ
οὔκουν ἔγωγε· φημὶ δ' οὔ σε μανθάνειν.

ΦΙΛΟΚΤΗΤΗΣ
ἐγὼ οὐκ Ἀτρείδας ἐκβαλόντας οἶδά με; 1390

ΝΕΟΠΤΟΛΕΜΟΣ
ἀλλ' ἐκβαλόντες εἰ πάλιν σώσουσ' ὅρα.

ΦΙΛΟΚΤΗΤΗΣ
οὐδέποθ' ἑκόντα γ' ὥστε τὴν Τροίαν ἰδεῖν.

ΝΕΟΠΤΟΛΕΜΟΣ
τί δῆτ' ἂν ἡμεῖς δρῶμεν, εἰ σέ γ' ἐν λόγοις
πείσειν δυνησόμεσθα μηδὲν ὧν λέγω;
ὡς ῥᾷστ' ἐμοὶ μὲν τῶν λόγων λῆξαι, σὲ δὲ 1395
ζῆν, ὥσπερ ἤδη ζῇς, ἄνευ σωτηρίας.

ΦΙΛΟΚΤΗΤΗΣ
ἔα με πάσχειν ταῦθ' ἅπερ παθεῖν με δεῖ·
ἃ δ' ᾔνεσάς μοι δεξιᾶς ἐμῆς θιγών,
πέμπειν πρὸς οἴκους, ταῦτά μοι πρᾶξον, τέκνον,
καὶ μὴ βράδυνε μηδ' ἐπιμνησθῇς ἔτι 1400
Τροίας· ἅλις γάρ μοι τεθρήνηται γόοις.

NEOPTOLEMUS

    For you, of course. I'm your friend. What I say
    is spoken in friendship.

PHILOCTETES

                How can that be true?
    You want to hand me to my enemies.

NEOPTOLEMUS

    My dear man, in such troubles you must learn
    not to be so stubborn.

PHILOCTETES

                You'll ruin me
    with these words of yours. I know that.

NEOPTOLEMUS

    No, I won't. But you don't understand—
    that's what I'm saying.

PHILOCTETES

            Don't I understand
    how those sons of Atreus threw me aside?   [1390]

NEOPTOLEMUS

    Yes, they cast you off, but you should see
    if they will rescue you again.

PHILOCTETES

               Never!
    Not if I must agree to go to Troy.

NEOPTOLEMUS

    What can I do then, if what I say
    will not convince you? The easiest thing
    for me is to say no more, and then you
    can go on living as you're doing now,
    without being rescued.

PHILOCTETES

            Let me keep suffering
    whatever I must suffer. But those things
    you swore to me, with your right hand in mine—
    to take me home—do that for me, my son,
    and don't hold back or keep reminding me   [1400]
    about Troy any more. I've had enough
    of howling lamentations here.

Sophocles

ΝΕΟΠΤΟΛΕΜΟΣ
εἰ δοκεῖ, στείχωμεν.

ΦΙΛΟΚΤΗΤΗΣ
ὦ γενναῖον εἰρηκὼς ἔπος.

ΝΕΟΠΤΟΛΕΜΟΣ
ἀντέρειδε νῦν βάσιν σήν.

ΦΙΛΟΚΤΗΤΗΣ
εἰς ὅσον γ᾽ ἐγὼ σθένω.

ΝΕΟΠΤΟΛΕΜΟΣ
αἰτίαν δὲ πῶς Ἀχαιῶν φεύξομαι;

ΦΙΛΟΚΤΗΤΗΣ
μὴ φροντίσῃς.

ΝΕΟΠΤΟΛΕΜΟΣ
τί γάρ, ἐὰν πορθῶσι χώραν τὴν ἐμήν;

ΦΙΛΟΚΤΗΤΗΣ
ἐγὼ παρὼν

ΝΕΟΠΤΟΛΕΜΟΣ
τίνα προσωφέλησιν ἔρξεις;   1405

ΦΙΛΟΚΤΗΤΗΣ
βέλεσι τοῖς Ἡρακλέους

ΝΕΟΠΤΟΛΕΜΟΣ
πῶς λέγεις;

ΦΙΛΟΚΤΗΤΗΣ
εἴρξω πελάζειν.

ΝΕΟΠΤΟΛΕΜΟΣ
στεῖχε προσκύσας χθόνα.

126

NEOPTOLEMUS

All right,
if that's what you truly want, let's leave.

PHILOCTETES

Ah, such noble words!

[PHILOCTETES starts to move down from his cave]

NEOPTOLEMUS

Plant your feet firmly.

PHILOCTETES

I will—as firmly as my strength allows.

NEOPTOLEMUS

How will I escape being blamed for this
by the Achaeans?

PHILOCTETES

Forget about those men.

NEOPTOLEMUS

What if they destroy my country?

PHILOCTETES

I'll be there . . .

NEOPTOLEMUS *[interrupting]*

What assistance will you give?

PHILOCTETES

. . . with these arrows
which come from Hercules . . .

NEOPTOLEMUS

What are you saying?

PHILOCTETES

I'll stop them coming in.

NEOPTOLEMUS

Then let's depart,
once you have bid your island home farewell.

[HERCULES appears above the stage][25]

127

Sophocles

ἩΡΑΚΛΗΣ
μήπω γε, πρὶν ἂν τῶν ἡμετέρων
ἀίῃς μύθων, παῖ Ποίαντος·
φάσκειν δ᾽ αὐδὴν τὴν Ἡρακλέους   1410
ἀκοῇ τε κλύειν λεύσσειν τ᾽ ὄψιν.
τὴν σὴν δ᾽ ἥκω χάριν οὐρανίας
ἕδρας προλιπών,
τὰ Διός τε φράσων βουλεύματά σοι   1415
κατερητύσων θ᾽ ὁδὸν ἣν στέλλει·
σὺ δ᾽ ἐμῶν μύθων ἐπάκουσον.
καὶ πρῶτα μέν σοι τὰς ἐμὰς λέξω τύχας,
ὅσους πονήσας καὶ διεξελθὼν πόνους
ἀθάνατον ἀρετὴν ἔσχον, ὡς πάρεσθ᾽ ὁρᾶν.   1420
καὶ σοί, σάφ᾽ ἴσθι, τοῦτ᾽ ὀφείλεται παθεῖν,
ἐκ τῶν πόνων τῶνδ᾽ εὐκλεᾶ θέσθαι βίον.
ἐλθὼν δὲ σὺν τῷδ᾽ ἀνδρὶ πρὸς τὸ Τρωικὸν
πόλισμα, πρῶτον μὲν νόσου παύσει λυγρᾶς,
ἀρετῇ τε πρῶτος ἐκκριθεὶς στρατεύματος,   1425
Πάριν μέν, ὃς τῶνδ᾽ αἴτιος κακῶν ἔφυ,
τόξοισι τοῖς ἐμοῖσι νοσφιεῖς βίου,
πέρσεις τε Τροίαν, σκῦλά τ᾽ εἰς μέλαθρα σὰ
πέμψεις, ἀριστεῖ᾽ ἐκλαβὼν στρατεύματος,
Ποίαντι πατρὶ πρὸς πάτρας Οἴτης πλάκα.   1430
ἃ δ᾽ ἂν λάβῃς σὺ σκῦλα τοῦδε τοῦ στρατοῦ,
τόξων ἐμῶν μνημεῖα πρὸς πυρὰν ἐμὴν
κόμιζε. καὶ σοὶ ταῦτ᾽, Ἀχιλλέως τέκνον,
παρήνεσ᾽· οὔτε γὰρ σὺ τοῦδ᾽ ἄτερ σθένεις
ἑλεῖν τὸ Τροίας πεδίον οὔθ᾽ οὗτος σέθεν.   1435
ἀλλ᾽ ὡς λέοντε συννόμω φυλάσσετον
οὗτος σὲ καὶ σὺ τόνδ᾽· ἐγὼ δ᾽ Ἀσκληπιὸν
παυστῆρα πέμψω σῆς νόσου πρὸς Ἴλιον.
τὸ δεύτερον γὰρ τοῖς ἐμοῖς αὐτὴν χρεὼν
τόξοις ἁλῶναι. τοῦτο δ᾽ ἐννοεῖθ᾽, ὅταν   1440
πορθῆτε γαῖαν, εὐσεβεῖν τὰ πρὸς θεούς·
ὡς τἄλλα πάντα δεύτερ᾽ ἡγεῖται πατὴρ
Ζεύς· οὐ γὰρ εὐσέβεια συνθνῄσκει βροτοῖς·
κἂν ζῶσι κἂν θάνωσιν, οὐκ ἀπόλλυται.

HERCULES
    Not yet, son of Poeas, not until you've heard
    the words that I shall utter. Know this—   [1410]
    you're listening to the voice of Hercules
    and you're gazing on his face. For your sake
    I have left the throne of heaven and come
    to announce to you the purposes of Zeus
    and to stop the journey you're proposing.
    So pay attention now to what I say.
    First, I will inform you of my exploits,
    for by struggling with so many labours
    and by seeing my work through to the end,
    I won immortal glory for myself,   [1420]
    as you can see. As for you, you must know
    it is your destiny that, from these troubles,
    you make your life something men honour.
    With this man you will reach the Trojan city,
    where, first, your savage illness will be cured,
    then you'll be chosen as the finest man
    from all the warriors, and with my bow,
    will cut short the life of Paris, the man
    who is the cause of all this wickedness.
    You will ransack Troy and from the army
    carry off the prize for utmost bravery,
    and take it home with you to Oeta,
    in your native mountains, to the great joy   [1430]
    of Poeas, your father. Whatever prizes
    you get from the army, select from them
    an offering for my bow and carry it
    to my funeral pyre. Son of Achilles,
    this advice I'm giving is for you, as well.
    You are not strong enough to capture Troy
    without this man, and he's not strong enough
    without you there. Like a pair of lions
    stalking prey on common ground, the two of you
    must guard each other's life. To cure your illness,
    I'll send Asclepius to Troy, which is doomed
    to fall a second time thanks to my arrows.[26]
    But remember this—when you lay waste that land,   [1440]
    show reverence to the gods, for Father Zeus
    thinks of all other things as less than that.
    And when men perish, piety does not—
    whether they're alive or dead, it does not die.

Sophocles

ΦΙΛΟΚΤΗΤΗΣ
ὦ φθέγμα ποθεινὸν ἐμοὶ πέμψας   1445
χρόνιός τε φανείς,
οὐκ ἀπιθήσω τοῖς σοῖς μύθοις.

ΝΕΟΠΤΟΛΕΜΟΣ
κἀγὼ γνώμην ταύτῃ τίθεμαι.

ἩΡΑΚΛΗΣ
μή νυν χρόνιοι μέλλετε πράσσειν·
καιρὸς καὶ πλοῦς   1450
ὅδ᾿ ἐπείγει γὰρ κατὰ πρύμνην.

ΦΙΛΟΚΤΗΤΗΣ
φέρε νυν στείχων χώραν καλέσω.
χαῖρ᾿, ὦ μέλαθρον ξύμφρουρον ἐμοί,
νύμφαι τ᾿ ἔνυδροι λειμωνιάδες,
καὶ κτύπος ἄρσην πόντου προβολῆς,
οὗ πολλάκι δὴ τοὐμὸν ἐτέγχθη
κρᾶτ᾿ ἐνδόμυχον πληγαῖσι νότου,
πολλὰ δὲ φωνῆς τῆς ἡμετέρας
Ἑρμαῖον ὄρος παρέπεμψεν ἐμοὶ
στόνον ἀντίτυπον χειμαζομένῳ.   1460
νῦν δ᾿, ὦ κρῆναι Λύκιόν τε ποτόν,
λείπομεν ὑμᾶς, λείπομεν ἤδη
δόξης οὔ ποτε τῆσδ᾿ ἐπιβάντες.
χαῖρ᾿, ὦ Λήμνου πέδον ἀμφίαλον,
καί μ᾿ εὐπλοίᾳ πέμψον ἀμέμπτως,
ἔνθ᾿ ἡ μεγάλη Μοῖρα κομίζει
γνώμη τε φίλων χὠ πανδαμάτωρ
δαίμων, ὃς ταῦτ᾿ ἐπέκρανεν.

ΧΟΡΟΣ
χωρῶμεν δὴ πάντες ἀολλεῖς,
νύμφαις ἁλίαισιν ἐπευξάμενοι   1470
νόστου σωτῆρας ἱκέσθαι.

130

Philoctetes

PHILOCTETES

O that voice I have longed to hear, my friend
who stands revealed to me after so long!
I will not disobey what you have said.

NEOPTOLEMUS

And I, too, will consent to this, as well.

HERCULES

Then do not spend a long time waiting here.
A stern wind will blow to urge you onward.   [1450]
The time is right to sail.

PHILOCTETES

                    All right, then,
let me salute this land as I depart.
Farewell, you cave that shared my vigil,
and farewell, you nymphs of streams and meadows,
you pounding headlands beaten by the sea,
where in the inner spaces of my den
the blasts from South Wind often soaked my head,
where Mount Hermaea often echoed   [1460]
the cries I screamed out in my storms of pain.
But now, you Lycian streams and waters,
I am leaving you, going away at last,
beyond all hopes I ever entertained.
Farewell, you sea-encircled land of Lemnos,
send me away content on a fair voyage,
to the place ordained by mighty Fate,
by opinions of my friends, and by the god
who conquers all and has brought this about.

CHORUS

Let's all leave in a group, once we have prayed
to the ocean nymphs, so they will come   [1470]
and guide us safely on our journey home.

[They all move off together]

NOTES

1. In the text below the speaking label CHORUS designates all speeches spoken by the Chorus collectively, the Chorus Leader, individual member of the Chorus, and special sub-groups of the entire Chorus. In any production of the play, the director would have to determine the speaker(s) for each speech.

2. The two commanders of the Argive expedition to Troy were the brothers Agamemnon and Menelaus.

3. Dardanus, a son of Zeus, was the legendary founder of Troy.

4. Many Greek warrior leaders had made an oath to assist whichever one of them was lucky enough to marry Helen, daughter of Tyndareus, king of Sparta, if he ever needed their help. When Paris of Troy abducted Helen, her husband, Menelaus, called upon the Achaean leaders to honour their promise by joining an expedition to attack Troy. Odysseus was very reluctant to join the expedition and had to be tricked into going.

5. The Achaean forces had learned by prophecy that they needed Neoptolemus and the bow of Philoctetes to capture Troy.

6. *Chryse* refers to the nymph who punished Philoctetes with the snake bite for desecrating her shrine. It is also the name of a small island close to Troy.

7. Cephallenia was an island in Odysseus' kingdom, but the name is often applied to his territory generally (and his soldiers are commonly called the Cephallenians).

8. Menelaus is king of Sparta, and Agamemnon is king of Mycenae. Neoptolemus was born and raised on the island of Scyros.

9. Sigeum was a prominent coastal location northwest of Troy.

10. Pactolus was a river in Asia Minor celebrated for its rich deposits of gold. The detail about lions slaughtering bulls seems to suggest (according to Jebb) that the goddess is riding on lions or that her throne is a chariot drawn by lions.

Sophocles

11. Sisyphus, the founder of Corinth, was famous for his devious ways. According to one story very popular among Odysseus' enemies, he was the father of Odysseus and sold his mother to Laertes while Odysseus was still in the womb. Diomedes was a close comrade of Odysseus.

12. Thersites, the only common soldier described in detail in Homer's *Iliad*, was well known for his abuse of his superiors. He gives a lengthy speech insulting Agamemnon.

13. Tydeus' son is a reference to the famous Greek warrior Diomedes, a frequent companion of Odysseus on various adventures.

14. The reference here is to Sisyphus who ordered his wife not to bury him. When he came to Hades, he complained about his wife's conduct and was given permission to go back to punish her. Once out of Hades, Sisyphus stayed on earth. Calling Sisyphus the father of Odysseus here is the second reference to the insulting story that Sisyphus sold Odysseus while he was still in his mother's womb to Laertes (see line 501 above).

15. The virtuous act Philoctetes is referring to is lighting the funeral pyre for Hercules.

16. The whirling wheel is a reference to Ixion, the first mortal charged with murder. Zeus pardoned his crime. But then Ixion attempted to seduce Zeus' wife Hera in her own bed. Zeus had Ixion tied onto a wheel of fire in Hades.

17. These lines are a reference to Hercules who was burned alive at his own request on top of Mount Oeta. Hercules was a mortal son of Zeus and, because of his amazing exploits, he was taken up into heaven as a god.

18. This is a reference to Hercules, who also suffered a great deal in life and had an agonizing death. Philoctetes is reminding Neoptolemus that whoever owns the bow seems to get punished by the gods who are jealous of any man's possessing such a weapon.

19. Lemnian fire, Jebb notes, seems to be a reference to a volcanic mountain called Mosuchlos on the east coast of Lemnos, near Philoctetes' cave. Hercules was taken up to the top of Mount Oeta by Hyllus, his son, who helped construct the pyre but would not set it alight. Philoctetes did so and, as a reward, got Hercules' bow.

20. The Chorus is advising Neoptolemus to take the bow and leave and thus abandon what he is presently intending (to take Philoctetes on board his ship). The trouble they are talking about is what might happen

on board once Philoctetes learns that he is going to Troy rather than back home. For them the easiest course seems to be to take the bow and abandon Philoctetes.

21. Philoctetes is contrasting his willingness to go along on the expedition to Troy with Odysseus' reluctance to join in. When the messenger came to enlist his support, Odysseus pretended to be mad, ploughing with an ox and an ass yoked together. The messenger placed Odysseus' infant son in front of the plough. Odysseus stopped before he could injure his son, thus revealing that his madness was a pretense.

22. Teucer, a character in Homer's *Iliad*, is one of the finest archers in the Greek forces. Archery is not normally a skill associated with the most important warriors, other than Odysseus (in the *Odyssey*).

23. This short speech of Odysseus is a conjecture based on Jebb's commentary to supply a line which is apparently missing from the manuscript.

24. Asclepius was the Greek hero (or god) associated with medicine. In the *Iliad*, his sons are the most important healers in the Greek forces at Troy.

25. This sudden appearance of a divine figure near the end of the play (the *deus ex machina*) may have had Hercules lowered from above or he may have appeared on a platform above the stage. Hercules was a mortal son of Zeus, but after his death he was made a god.

26. Hercules himself had in earlier times attacked the king of Troy, Laomedon, and captured the city.